Arts and Disabled People

Report of a Committee of Inquiry
under the Chairmanship of
Sir Richard Attenborough

Published for
Carnegie UK Trust by
BEDFORD SQUARE PRESS|NCVO

Published by
BEDFORD SQUARE PRESS of the
National Council for Voluntary Organisations
26 Bedford Square, London WC1B 3HU

ISBN 0 7199 1145 1

First published 1985

Typeset by Auckland Litho, 5-25 Burr Road, Wandsworth, London SW18 4SG
Printed and bound in England by
Latimer Trend & Company Ltd, Plymouth

Contents

The Carnegie United Kingdom Trust wishes to place on record its gratitude to the Chairman, Vice-Chairman and members of the Committee of Inquiry, and to the Committee's staff, for all they have done in the course of their proceedings, including work on the studies they initiated, culminating in the drawing up of this report.

The Trustees join with the Committee in extending their sincere thanks to all who have given financial support to the Inquiry.

List of Members

The following were appointed by the Carnegie United Kingdom Trust to form the Committee of Inquiry into the Arts and Disabled People:

CHAIRMAN:
Sir Richard Attenborough CBE

VICE-CHAIRMAN:
★Sir Alec Atkinson KCB DFC
Former Second Permanent Secretary, Department of Health and Social Security

SECRETARY:
★Geoffrey Lord
Secretary and Treasurer, Carnegie United Kingdom Trust

MEMBERS:
Alexander Dunbar
Former Director, Scottish Arts Council
James Ford-Smith OBE
Public Relations Officer, Ulster Museum; Vice-Chairman, Northern Ireland Council for the Handicapped
★Gordon Infield
Charity Manager, Marks and Spencer plc
Sue Jennings
Senior Lecturer in Dramatherapy
★Daphne Kennard MBE
Music Adviser, Disabled Living Foundation
Pat Keysell
Founder and Director of the former British Theatre of the Deaf; Mime artist in residence
Baroness Lane-Fox OBE
Chairman, Phipps Respiratory Unit Patients Association; Chairman, Thames TV Telethon 1985
Gina Levete MBE
Founder of Shape and Interlink
★Bert Massie OBE
Executive Assistant to the Director of the Royal Association for Disability and Rehabilitation
John Oliver
National Officer, National Federation of Gateway Clubs
Brian Rix CBE
Secretary-General, Royal Society for Mentally Handicapped Adults and Children

★Peter Senior
Director, Manchester Hospitals' Arts Project; Senior Lecturer in Art and Design, Manchester Polytechnic
Veronica Sherborne
Senior Lecturer in Movement, Bristol Polytechnic
Paul Walker
Executive Director, Muscular Dystrophy Group of Great Britain and Northern Ireland
Elinor Bennett Wigley
Member of All-Wales Panel for Development of Services for Mentally Handicapped People

OBSERVERS:
Rod Fisher
Information Officer, Arts Council of Great Britain
Simon Goodenough
Educational publisher and author
Rodney Stone
(until January 1983)
Assistant Secretary, Office of Arts and Libraries
Hilary Bauer
(from January to July 1983)
Principal, Office of Arts and Libraries
Derek Lodge
(from July 1983)
Principal, Office of Arts and Libaries
Patricia Winterton
(until June 1984)
Assistant Secretary, Department of Health and Social Security (DHSS)
Nick Boyd
(from June 1984)
Principal, Community Services Division, DHSS

PROJECT DIRECTOR:
★Carolyn Keen

ASSISTANT:
Gillian McWilliams
(until August 1984)
Ruth Freedman
(from August 1984)

PROJECT OFFICER:
★Christina McDonald

ASSISTANT:
Irene Ure

(★These members and officers served on the Management Sub-Committee)

v

Acknowledgements

This Inquiry was set up by the Carnegie United Kingdom Trust which has provided the main support for it.

The Committee appointed to conduct the Inquiry wishes gratefully to acknowledge this support and also the assistance received from the staff of the Trust, from the Regional Arts Associations and from many other organisations and individuals. In particular, the Committee wishes to thank those who have made financial contributions, submitted evidence, or helped in one way or another with the 16 consultative meetings held in different parts of the United Kingdom. In this and other connections, especial thanks for their involvement are due to the Minister for the Arts, Lord Gowrie, and to the Minister for the Disabled, Tony Newton OBE MP.

Those who have made financial contributions to the Inquiry, and the projects connected with it, include:

Office of Arts and Libraries
Arts Council of Great Britain
Allen Lane Foundation
Baring Foundation
Chase Charity
City Parochial Foundation
Ernest Cook Trust
Esmée Fairbairn Charitable
    Trust
Hayward Foundation
Royal Wedding Fund
Wates Foundation
Marks and Spencer
Shell UK Ltd

Those who have contributed towards the cost of the 16 consultative meetings include:

Arts Council of Northern Ireland
British Petroleum
Cambridge City Council
Dyfed County Council
City of Glasgow District Council
Newcastle City Council
Reading Borough Council
Scunthorpe Borough Council
South Glamorgan County
    Council
University of Leicester
and
12 Regional Arts Associations in
    England
3 Regional Arts Associations in
    Wales

The Committee wishes to express its thanks to the Director of the British Museum, Sir David Wilson, for agreeing to second Anne Pearson to prepare guidance notes 'Arts for Everyone'; her work has proved invaluable. The Committee also thanks Hugh Spencely and Sarah Langton-Lockton, the Chairman and the Director of the Centre on Environment for the Handicapped, for the leading part they have played in advancing the project.

The Committee is grateful to Dr Peter Coles, for preparing an evaluation of the British Museum's 'Please Touch' Exhibition; to Peter Cox, for chairing a group on the evaluation of projects; to Dr Ken Robinson for looking after the drafting of the chapter on Arts Education and Training (Chapter 9) and for other help; to Valerie Nimmo and Teresa Wallace for their voluntary work on the survey of arts venues in Edinburgh; and to the seven Marks and Spencer management trainees who made a survey of arts publicity in seven towns and cities.

Most of the administrative and other work connected with the Inquiry has been performed by the Committee's staff, comprising Carolyn Keen in London, Christina McDonald in Dunfermline and their respective assistants, Gillian McWilliams (succeeded in August 1984 by Ruth Freedman) and Irene Ure. They have worked under the general supervision of Geoffrey Lord, Secretary to the Carnegie United Kingdom Trust, who has acted also as Secretary to the Committee. Each has shown entire commitment to the purposes of the Inquiry and the Committee is glad to place on record its grateful recognition.

The Committee is indebted also to the organisations and individuals who have assisted the staff by providing facilities or help; these include the Central Office of Information, the International Press-Cutting Bureau, the Polytechnic of North London (Survey Research Unit) and, among individuals, Valerie Blackborn, Barbie Boxall, Keith Howes, Jean Reneson Keen, Lynne Martin, and Michael Regan.

For most of the time, the Committee has been based in Nuffield Lodge and its warm thanks are due to the Nuffield Foundation and to the Foundation's staff for a friendly welcome and for many kindnesses. The Committee is also much indebted to IBM United Kingdom Ltd for providing accommodation at the start of the Inquiry and for word-processing equipment; to the Horace Moore Charitable Trust and Project Office Equipment Ltd for generous help with equipment; and to Marks and Spencer for providing excellent facilities for the Committee's meetings.

There are many other organisations and individuals who have been of great assistance; the Committee can only thank them collectively and gratefully acknowledge that without their support it would not have been practicable to carry through the Inquiry or complete this report.

Preface

The performing arts, in general, are principally the focus of my working days, and in my leisure hours I have long been concerned with the needs of disabled people. With these twin interests, therefore, I expected, when I first joined this Inquiry, to be traversing largely familiar ground. It has proved otherwise. I have learned of a whole new range of imaginative initiatives and these, in their turn, have served to point the way towards almost limitless further possibilities for involving disabled people in artistic pursuits.

Anyone who studies this area will find that it has been lamentably neglected by bodies, both national and local, well placed to take the lead. The Parliamentary All-Party Disablement Committee has given us strong encouragement. In 1982, however, the needs of disabled people were shamefully, almost totally, ignored by the Education, Science and Arts Committee of the House of Commons in their major report on 'Public and Private Funding of the Arts'. Information from bodies providing grants and donations indicates support for disability in general, but little emphasis so far on involvement in the arts. The Carnegie Trustees, together with the other supporters of this Inquiry, believe in the initiatives being taken, limited though they may be, and in the opportunities available. They are convinced as to the need and value of the arts and crafts to improve the quality of life for those with a disability. Additional practical support is vital, and I hope that more influential people and organisations, despite their other priorities and problems, will be convinced and encourage increased resources for accessibility and activities.

What is needed now is a vision and a plan. In our different ways, all of us engaged in this Inquiry have seen the vision, and in our report we have tried to set out a plan. It is a plan defined largely in the unemotional language of administration, but those who work to implement it will surely find themselves led on by the vision that we have seen.

As the move forward gathers pace, new possibilities will begin to emerge. The ultimate target must be to enable and encourage disabled people to play the fullest possible part in the artistic life of the community. We cannot know when, or precisely how, that will be achieved, but we can make a determined move in the right direction. Our report is designed to chart the way. It lies within the power of our generation to transform the lives of disabled people and to enrich the world of art itself by their greater involvement. Failure to act diminishes us all.

January 1985

Summary of recommend-ations

The following is a summary of the main recommendations contained in this report:*

Access to the arts

The *Secretary of State for the Environment* should now proceed with the making of building regulations (applicable to new buildings and to major alterations and extensions) under which, in all arts buildings for public use, there would have to be provision for access by disabled people to and within all floors and a reasonable number of suitable toilets. *(Chapter 4.11)*

The *Home Secretary* should initiate a review of the arrangements for licensing public buildings, to be conducted with the help of disabled people's organisations. Two of the main objects would be to provide clearer guidance for fire officers and to devise a national code of practice designed to promote positive attitudes towards disabled people both by those

*Apart from recommendations applicable specifically to Northern Ireland, Scotland and Wales, the summary has been prepared in terms appropriate to English constitutional and administrative arrangements, but the intention is that the same principles should apply throughout the United Kingdom.

who administer licences and by the managers of arts venues. *(Chapter 4.13)*

The *Minister for the Arts* should make funds available for adapting arts venues within his Departmental responsibility to make them more accessible to disabled people, and the *Minister for the Disabled* should co-ordinate the making of corresponding arrangements in relation to other arts venues. *(Chapter 4.17)*

Owners of arts venues should ensure that their managers have clear instructions on the admission of disabled people, based on a presumption of access, and should provide for adequate training of all staff on ways of helping disabled people. *(Chapter 4.42)*

National Access Committees should review the arrangements for recording and disseminating information about access to arts venues, and should consider experimenting with registration systems. *(Chapter 5.32)*

National Access Committees should arrange for the setting up of a working group to prepare guidelines on ticket concessions for disabled people at arts venues. *(Chapter 4.50)*

The *Secretary of State for Transport* should consider means of fostering the best development of schemes for helping disabled people get to and from arts venues. *(Chapter 4.54)*

Sub-titling of films

The *British Film Institute* should promote the building up of a comprehensive library of sub-titled films available for hiring. *(Chapter 4.30)*

Arts Council policy

The *Arts Council*★ should each, within a year (a) publish a policy statement committing themselves to widening the arts opportunities of disabled people, and stating how they will seek to achieve this, and the means by which they will expect their clients to do so; (b) make it a condition for funding that arts enterprises take adequate steps to serve the needs of disabled people in their employment policies, in their access facilities, in their educational programmes and in their publicity; and (c) include in their policy statements an account of their criteria for meeting requests for funding from arts companies wishing to work with disabled people and from groups which include disabled artists. *(Chapter 5.4 to 5.8)*

★The Arts Councils comprise the Arts Council of Great Britain including the Scottish and Welsh Arts Councils, and the Arts Council of Northern Ireland.

Regional Arts Association policies

Each *Regional Arts Association* should, within a year, issue a policy statement relating to participation by disabled people, and should make it a condition of funding that proper consideration is being given to meeting the needs of such people. *(Chapter 5.11 to 5.16)*

Policy statements by other bodies disbursing funds for arts purposes

Policy statements relating to arts opportunities for disabled people should be published also by *other bodies concerned with the disbursement of funds for arts purposes*, including government departments, local authorities, charitable trusts and commercial sponsors. In settling the conditions under which they will fund arts projects, these bodies should take into account the extent to which the needs of disabled people will be met. *(Chapter 5.19 and 5.20)*

Policy statements by professional organisations

Professional and other organisations whose members are concerned with arts activities should make policy statements on arts opportunities for disabled people. *(Chapter 5.21)*

Crafts

The *Crafts Council* should make a policy statement committing itself to provide special help for disabled people and this extension of the Council's activities should be taken into account in the allocation of funds to it. *(Chapter 5.22)*

Arts clubs and societies

The *national councils of organisations concerned with amateur involvement in arts activities* should issue guidance to their members on how best they can enable and encourage disabled people to join. *(Chapter 5.23)*

National disability organisations

National disability organisations with a network of local clubs should consider means of enabling selected club leaders and helpers to attend training courses in the arts, and means of making available to members of their clubs specialist advice on, and training in, arts activities. *(Chapter 5.24)*

Integrated arts workshops by professional touring companies

Co-ordinating organisations such as the *Regional Arts Associations* and *Shape services* should help touring companies to make arrangements locally for arts workshops involving disabled people. *(Chapter 5.25)*

Consultative meetings

Starting within a year, *Regional Arts Associations* (in conjunction with other co-ordinating services) should take the lead in organising consultative meetings on the expansion of arts opportunities for disabled people. Such meetings should be the start of a regular series of meetings to be held at least once every two years. *(Chapter 5.27)*

Lists of disability organisations

Disability organisations and arts organisations should together draw up regional lists of those disability organisations which should be informed when there are vacancies to be filled on the management committees of arts bodies. *(Chapter 5.36)*

Assignment of responsibilities within local authorities

The *Chief Executive of each local authority* should ensure that the subject of disability is discussed in the management group and that there is a clear allocation of responsibility within the authority relating to arts provision for disabled people. *(Chapter 6.10)*

National Health Service

The *Secretary of State for Social Services* should require Regional and District Health Authorities to develop the use of the arts and to establish programmes for utilising the services of artists. *(Chapter 6.19)*

District Health Authorities should each designate an officer to be responsible for co-ordinating the provision of arts opportunities and for developing relevant arts programmes within the authority. *(Chapter 6.22)*

The brief for any new hospital or redevelopment should include the provision of works of art and of facilities for arts activities. *(Chapter 6.25)*

Arts therapies

The *Secretary of State for Social Services* and the *Secretary of State for Education and Science* should (a) each designate an officer to liaise with relevant professional and statutory bodies on the development of arts therapies; and (b) jointly initiate a comprehensive review of the arrangements for the practice of arts therapies. Among the objects of the review should be to provide a specification for a national consultative committee for the arts and arts therapies; to work out arrangements for health, education and social services authorities jointly to appoint a qualified arts therapies officer at senior level; to prepare plans for

District Health Authorities, in conjunction with the social services, to set up multi-disciplinary teams, comprising arts therapists and other artists, to service hospitals, clinics, special schools, day centres and community settings; to devise a scheme for ensuring that courses in the medical and caring professions, and relevant educational courses, have some input from the arts including arts therapies, and that arts training courses consider arts therapies. *(Chapter 7.18)*

The *associations concerned with arts therapies* should (a) consider means of disseminating more information about the work of arts therapists; and (b) combine together to provide a forum for an exchange of views and to establish joint seminars. *(Chapter 7.19)*

All *organisations for disabled people* , and particularly organisations concerned with the provision and quality of care in institutions, should designate an officer to be responsible for the arts, including arts therapies. *(Chapter 7.20)*

Libraries

The *Minister for the Arts* should seek the setting up of a small unit to serve as an information and advice centre on library services for disabled people; should invite the Library and Information Services Council to consider developments in the library services relating to disabled people; and should include an account of important developments in his annual report to Parliament on the library service. *(Chapter 8.23)*

All *library authorities* should review their services for disabled people to see what improvements can be made, and should take particular account of the needs of mentally handicapped people. *(Chapter 8.24)*

The *Library Association* should (a) prepare policy statements on library provision for disabled people living in the community and on library employment opportunities for disabled people; and (b) take all practicable steps to ensure that in library schools and library training sessions proper account is taken of the needs of disabled people, including those who are mentally handicapped. *(Chapter 8.25)*

Public libraries should maintain contact with local disability groups and invite members of these groups to staff training sessions. *(Chapter 8.26)*

Education and training

All ordinary schools should formulate a policy for educating disabled children which covers (a) means of identifying children with physical or mental disabilities, and of establishing their abilities; (b) ways of modifying teaching methods and resources to meet the needs of such children; and (c) provision for regular meetings between staff from the different arts disciplines to make time-table adjustments to meet the needs of such children. *(Chapter 9.23 to 9.26)*

Local education authorities should take urgent action to arrange for training which (a) for all arts teachers in ordinary schools, deals with the identification of children who have special educational needs and, in the initial training of such teachers, covers the adaptation of teaching techniques and uses of equipment for these children; and (b) for all teachers being trained for work in special schools, covers the purposes of the arts in education. Corresponding action should be taken by organisations responsible for the management of schools in the voluntary sector. *(Chapter 9.31 and 9.32)*

The *education advisory services* should explore ways of exchanging expertise between arts departments and special schools by a system of school partnerships. *(Chapter 9.34)*

Institutions running further education courses in the arts should (a) ensure that their prospectuses provide relevant information to applicants with disabilities and are sent as appropriate to specialist Careers Officers for the handicapped and to the Manpower Services Commission for the use of Disablement Resettlement Officers; (b) foster stronger links between students, careers advisers, Disablement

Resettlement Officers and disability organisations such as the National Bureau for Handicapped Students, so that information on arts opportunities in further education can be collated for the benefit of intending students. (*Chapter 9.39*)

Colleges for higher education in the arts should (a) avoid taking employment prospects into account in deciding whether to admit disabled people to courses; (b) have a published policy on the admission and support of disabled students, drawn up after discussion among staff and students; (c) include disability on the agenda of the governing body at least once a year; and (d) ensure that their internal assessment and examination arrangements can be adapted to the needs of disabled students. (*Chapter 9.46 and 9.47, and 9.50*)

The *Secretary of State for Education and Science* should establish a special fund on which institutions accepting disabled students for higher education in the arts could draw for any necessary adaptations of their facilities. (*Chapter 9.48*)

Agencies involved with disability should seek ways of collaborating, on a regional basis, with the providers of adult education and with arts funding bodies to enable and encourage disabled adults to take advantage of educational opportunities in the arts. (*Chapter 9.56*)

National Centres for the Training of Teachers for Further and Technical Education should include courses on the place of the arts in the education of students with special needs. (*Chapter 9.60*)

Organisations responsible for training arts administrators should cover in their courses the handicapping effects of disabilities and strategies for overcoming them. (*Chapter 9.61*)

National *Access Committees* should encourage arts organisations to initiate short training courses for managers and staff of arts venues on ways of meeting the needs of disabled people. (*Chapter 4.43*)

Manpower Services Commission

The *Secretary of State for Employment* should establish with the Manpower Services Commission (a) the best means of extending arts training and arts employment opportunities for disabled people; and (b) how the Commission's programmes can be used most effectively to improve access facilities at arts venues. (*Chapter 10.22*)

The *Manpower Services Commission* should seek to ensure that arts-related schemes brought to it by sponsors will be accessible to disabled people and that this will be made clear in each project's publicity. (*Chapter 10.22*)

Code of employment practice

All *arts employers* and all *professional associations with members in arts employment* should formally adhere to the Code of Good Practice for Employment of Disabled People drawn up by the Manpower Services Commission. *(Chapter 10.23)*

Insurance for disabled performers

Representatives of *employers and trade unions* should discuss with insurance companies any difficulties experienced in securing adequate insurance cover for disabled performers. *(Chapter 10.28)*

Policy statements by trade unions

All *trade unions* with members in the performing arts should promulgate policies for maximising the employment of disabled people and the TUC should give a lead on this to member unions. *(Chapter 10.29)*

Policy statements by the BBC and the IBA

The *British Broadcasting Corporation* and the *Independent Broadcasting Authority* should publish policy statements on the involvement of disabled people in their programmes. *(Chapter 10.34)*

Northern Ireland, Scotland and Wales

The *Association of Local Authorities of Northern Ireland* should initiate discussions with arts promoters, disabled people and leisure centre managers to encourage the growth of arts activities in leisure centres and the full participation of disabled people. *(Chapter 11.3)*

The *Northern Ireland Council for the Handicapped* should bring together interested organisations and individuals to plan a three-year pilot scheme for building on existing initiatives for use of the arts in work with handicapped people. *(Chapter 11.16 and 11.17)*

Area Boards in Northern Ireland should ensure that funds are available to enable the Liaison Officers for the Voluntary Sector to co-ordinate arts provision. *(Chapter 11.18)*

The *Convention of Scottish Local Authorities* should arrange a meeting to seek ways of increasing the involvement of its members in promoting the arts with disabled people. *(Chapter 11.28)*

The *Scottish Arts Council* should establish a series of priorities for arts funding involving disabled people, in consultation with the Scottish Council on Disability Committee on Arts for Scotland (SCD Committee on Arts for

Scotland) and other arts and disability organisations. *(Chapter 11.33)*

The *SCD Committee on Arts for Scotland*, in consultation with arts organisations and organisations for disabled people, should draw up a list of priorities for work by the Scottish Council on Disability directed to improving the arts opportunities for disabled people. *(Chapter 11.34)*

The *Scottish Hospital Advisory Service*, in conjunction with the SCD Committee on Arts for Scotland and the Scottish Arts Council, should plan a substantial arts development in a long stay hospital. *(Chapter 11.37)*

The *Secretary of State for Scotland* should arrange for the Scottish education system to be examined in the light of the principles set out in Chapter 9 of the report with a view to announcing a policy on the arts education of disabled people in Scotland. *(Chapter 11.41)*

The *Secretary of State for Wales* should arrange for a thorough reappraisal of the allocation of resources in Wales for helping disabled people to become more fully involved in arts activities; the organisations brought into consultation should include the Welsh Arts Council, Regional Arts Associations and representatives of voluntary organisations. *(Chapter 11.49)*

Chapter 1

Introduction

1.1 We were appointed by the Carnegie United Kingdom Trust to look into the extent to which existing facilities enable people with disabilities to involve themselves in the arts, whether as artists or audience, and to make recommendations to encourage development and improvement. Each of us has served on the committee in an individual capacity. Our report in no way commits organisations with which particular members are associated, nor have the observers who sat in on our proceedings any responsibility at all for the policies proposed or views expressed.

1.2 Our report explains how we have conducted the Inquiry, describes some of the things we have found, and sets out our recommendations. The need for action on these recommendations is urgent. The report should therefore be of particular and immediate concern to those to whom our recommendations are directed, but we hope that it will be read also by everyone who already is, or can be encouraged to become, interested in the subject of our Inquiry.

Meaning and importance of 'the arts'

1.3 We have used the term 'arts' in this report to include 'crafts'. Among the wide range of activities we have considered are:- dance, drama, film, puppetry, music, mime, movement, story-telling, drawing, painting, sculpture, pottery, photography and literature, as well as museum and library services.

1.4 A conviction that the arts are of profound value has been fundamental to our approach. The case for the arts can be presented in many different ways and at various levels of sophistication but the following simple points often find a place.

1.5 First, there is the pleasure the arts can bring both to those who practise the arts and to those who observe or listen. The unique quality - and frequently the intensity - of the pleasure must in part derive from the way in which the arts can reflect and develop a person's own experience and view of the world.

1.6 Second, there is the heightened sense of identity and individual worth that results from the uncovering of hidden talents and skills, whether of performance or of appreciation;

from the creation of beauty or fresh insights; and from finding an outlet for one's own innermost thoughts, feelings and beliefs.

1.7 Third, there is the sense of community that comes from the sustained endeavour in the arts to share ideas, emotions and experiences; to explore with others new combinations of shape, texture and colour, sound and rhythm; and even to extend, by however modest a margin, the area of human understanding.

1.8 Fourth, there is the contribution the arts can make to the development of various physical and perceptual skills.

1.9 The arts should never be regarded as open only to a privileged élite. The arts are for everyone. To some degree, it is within everyone's capacity to re-interpret their own experience, and to share the experience of others, by involvement in the world of art. Over the ages, the arts have been the field for and have prompted some of the finest achievements of the human spirit.

1.10 Active involvement is best of all, where people, as individuals or in a group, are themselves engaged in creating something. But absorption in the work of other artists, in whatever medium, can itself be a creative act. The arts have to be worked at, and thought about, and the results can sometimes be very disturbing. But the rewards and satisfactions should be there for all to secure, in whatever way is best suited to each person's individual interests and circumstances.

Professional and amateur arts

1.11 Our report covers both the professional arts and the amateur arts - that is, cases where artists are paid for practising their art more or less as a full-time occupation, and cases where art is a leisure-time activity rather than a means of livelihood. The distinction between the two categories may sometimes be blurred, but the professional artist usually has significantly more training, experience and skill than the amateur.

1.12 There are important implications for funding bodies insofar as, in the professional arts, the cost of remuneration has to be added to the cost of meeting the needs which professional and amateur artists have in common - space, equipment, facilities, training, and opportunities to practise. Some disabled people are, or want to become, professional artists or performers. Others want to participate in amateur arts activities as well as to form part of the audience for professional and amateur arts. The policies of funding bodies need to be flexible enough to provide an appropriate response in each case.

2

Meaning of 'disabled people'

1.13 We have taken a broad view of who, for the purposes of our remit, should be regarded as 'disabled people', and have had regard to the definition of 'disability' used by the World Health Organisation:- 'Any restriction or lack (resulting from an impairment) of ability to perform an activity in the manner or within the range considered normal for a human being'. Thus we have been concerned not only with the needs of people who are totally or partially blind or deaf, or who are in some other way physically impaired, but also with the needs of those who are mentally ill or mentally handicapped, or whose speech is impaired, or who have hidden handicaps resulting from conditions such as epilepsy or due to ageing. The term 'impairment', on which the definition of disability rests, is defined by the World Health Organisation as:- 'Any loss or abnormality of psychological, physiological, or anatomical structure or function'.

1.14 It has been brought home to us from the outset that there are no universally accepted terms in which to discuss the subject of our Inquiry. In this report, we talk about 'disabled people' rather than 'the disabled' as better reflecting our conviction that the humanity all hold in common is of more fundamental importance than any differentiation by reference to physical or mental capacity. Some believe that the term 'handicapped people' is better but we have decided to keep to the term 'disabled people', which accords with the terminology used in the International Year of Disabled People. The term 'handicap' we use to mean 'the loss or limitation of opportunities to take part in the life of the community on an equal level with others'; this is the sense in which the term is employed under the *World Programme of Action concerning Disabled Persons*, adopted by the United Nations in 1983.[1] In some contexts the terms 'disability' and 'handicap' are virtually interchangeable, but 'handicap', on the definition we have adopted, is always a function of the relationship between disabled people and their environment.

Numbers of disabled people

1.15 In *Designing for the Disabled*[2] Selwyn Goldsmith estimated, on the basis of the survey conducted by Amelia Harris in 1968, that nearly 8 per cent of the population of the United Kingdom suffered some handicap or impairment. At 12 per cent, Professor Peter Townsend's estimate of the numbers of disabled and long-term sick was even higher.[3] On the other hand, Outset, founded in 1970 to carry out full identification surveys of handicapped people, has estimated that about 4 per cent of the population are sufficiently disabled to suffer a long-term disadvantage which adversely affects their capacity to achieve the personal and economic independence normal for people of their age and sex.[4] The large variation in these estimates owes a great deal to differences of definition, and it is clear that the Outset definition (no doubt correctly for its own purposes) excludes many elderly people whose access to, or enjoyment of, the arts is liable to be adversely affected by mental or physical disablement - and who would therefore be within the scope of our Inquiry.

1.16 We welcome the Government's announcement of an intention to collect fuller statistics about disabled people. Even so, there is already clear evidence that the numbers coming within the scope of our Inquiry are very substantial indeed and likely to become even greater with the prospect of a further increase in the average age of the population. We have been accustomed to think in terms of one disabled person in every ten of the population and of one in four families having a disabled member. Until better information is available, these figures may be taken to indicate the broad orders of magnitude involved, though they are almost certainly too low to cover everyone with a significant hearing impairment - indeed, this group by itself may, on some

definitions, constitute as much as one-tenth of the population and include some six million people, or perhaps substantially more.

Value of the arts to disabled people

1.17 Some people have suggested that, instead of the task assigned to us, it would have been better had we been charged to study means of satisfying more fully the material needs of disabled people. We understand this point of view but we do not share it. We cannot accept that, as is sometimes said, the arts are no more than the 'icing on the cake'. Such a description pays scant regard to the central place the arts can hold in many lives. The arts offer not only diversion and enjoyment but can provide insights into the human condition and environment not achievable in any other way. Whether the arts are pursued primarily for their entertainment value or at a deeper level - and apart from their use specifically for therapeutic purposes - their importance can be even greater for people whose outlets are restricted by physical, mental or sensory impairment, than for other members of the community.

1.18 Disabled people are involved across the whole spectrum of artistic activity. There are those who pursue literary or other arts activities not directly affected by their particular disablement. Others engage in arts activities which, on a superficial view, might seem to be precluded for them - actors who are confined to wheelchairs, painters or photographers who are totally blind, musical performers who are profoundly deaf. By involvement in the arts, and sometimes indeed by developing their own art forms out of their own view and experience of life, people with very severe disablements have ceased to think of themselves as inadequate people compared with the able-bodied, and have come to recognise that they have their own particular contribution to make.

One of the plaintive comments from IYDP: a reminder of the need to heed views and wishes of those with a disability.

Preparations for the Inquiry and factors relevant to its timing

1.19 The general plans for our Inquiry were laid by a small steering group whose members, with one exception, were then able to accept appointment to our committee. Earlier on, the ground had been explored in a preliminary way at two national seminars arranged by the Carnegie United Kingdom Trust - one at Dartington in 1978 and the other in Stirling in 1979.[5]

1.20 Our Inquiry has been concerned with disabled people in all sorts of different circumstances and in every age group, from the young to the very old. There are two factors, however, which have made the Inquiry particularly timely. The first is that the present high totals of unemployed people include a disproportionately large number who are disabled. The second is that people are more likely to be affected by disablement as they get older, and the ratio of pensioners to working population, which has grown very substantially in recent decades, has not yet reached its peak.

General theme of the report

1.21 In the course of our investigations, we have found many examples of artistic ability allied with personal qualities which have enabled disabled people to achieve much in the practice of the arts. We have found that progress has been

5

made in rendering the arts accessible to disabled people in ways which would hardly have seemed possible 25 years ago. We have encountered much devoted and skilful work with disabled people in artistic endeavour. Yet an enormous task remains. There are still far too many areas of the arts inaccessible to disabled people, and still vast numbers of disabled people who are being starved of arts opportunities. In this report we have tried to chart the way forward so that the present frustrations of disabled people can increasingly be overcome. No-one who examined the evidence we have received could doubt the need.

How the report is organised

1.22 The next chapter of the report relates to the Committee's method of work, and to some of the studies initiated. The report goes on to discuss the present involvement of disabled people in the arts, and ways in which greater opportunities could be provided. Subsequent chapters deal with particular aspects of the Inquiry, and the report ends with some brief reflections on the Committee's findings and recommendations.

1.23 The 10 Appendices to the report provide supporting information, particularly on the studies undertaken, including a list of organisations which have given evidence (Appendix 1) and the addresses of some of the link organisations concerned with the provision of arts opportunities for disabled people (Appendix 2).

1.24 The principles behind our recommendations are intended to apply throughout the United Kingdom. Where there might otherwise be doubt as to the means of application in Northern Ireland, Scotland and Wales an explanation is given. A separate chapter is also devoted to these countries.

1.25 References are provided where appropriate at the end of each chapter, and where further reading is recommended on the related topic.

References

1 United Nations Report.
World Programme of Action concerning Disabled Persons, United Nations, New York, 1983

2 Goldsmith, Selwyn.
Designing for the Disabled, RIBA Publications, 1976

3 Townsend, Peter.
Poverty in the United Kingdom, Penguin Press, 1979

4 Outset.
Paradigm of Handicap, Outset, London 1984

5 Lord, Geoffrey.
The Arts and Disabilities, Macdonald Publishers, Edinburgh, 1981

Chapter 2

Procedure and studies undertaken

2.1 From our first full meeting on 15 September 1982 to our last on 22 October 1984, we have met as a full Committee on nine occasions. In between meetings the impetus has been maintained by a management committee, the composition of which is shown on the list of committee members which precedes our report. The management committee has met 12 times.

2.2 From the outset, we made great efforts to ensure that interested organisations and individuals would know of our Inquiry. Over 3,000 copies of press notices were sent out to the media and to many different organisations, and use was made also of magazine articles and of radio and television interviews. In March 1983, letters were sent to some 800 organisations inviting them to provide us with information and, as necessary, to nominate someone to liaise with us. In March 1984, a further letter about the provision of evidence was sent to over 300 of these organisations. In the result, over 300 organisations provided us with evidence (Appendix 1);

our staff also had extensive correspondence with individuals, thus enabling us to take account of their views. One of our main concerns has been to learn from the experience of disabled people not in touch with relevant organisations. In May 1984, our Chairman sent a letter to the national press inviting individuals to let us have their views. Nearly 300 replies were received and a response was sent to each.

Regional consultative meetings

2.3 We decided early on that we should arrange a series of consultative meetings, to be held in different parts of the country. We hoped in this way to stimulate interest in the subject of our Inquiry and to encourage discussion and collaboration between arts organisations and organisations for disabled people. The meetings were designed to assist us in appraising the existing situation, and in identifying promising lines of development. Having a series of meetings of this sort was a new departure and we intended that it should act as a catalyst for further action on similar lines. In arranging and running these meetings we were fortunate enough to secure the co-operation of the 15 Regional Arts Associations in England and Wales, and the Arts Council of Northern Ireland. We also had the support of the Scottish Arts Council for our meeting in Glasgow.

_ "IF YOU'LL JUST HANG ON A 'MO' WHILST I GET OUT OF THIS MESS, THEN I'LL GIVE YOU A HAND!" _

An early wry comment on the committee's progress following one of the regional meetings.

2.4 In the course of six months, 16 consultative meetings were held, each attended by between about 80 and 250 people. The meetings were in Belfast, Bristol, Cambridge, Cardiff, Carmarthen, Glasgow, Leeds, Leicester, London, Manchester, Mold, Newcastle, Reading, Scunthorpe, Stafford and Tonbridge. They brought together representatives of a wide range of statutory and non-statutory bodies, as well as people attending in an individual capacity. Speakers were invited who could help to illuminate the various issues from a national or a regional standpoint.

2.5 A report of these meetings was prepared by our staff, and circulated, summarising the matters discussed and the recommendations which emerged. We have taken these recommendations into account when formulating our own. Some further information about the meetings is given in Appendix 3.

Studies initiated by the Committee

2.6 Throughout our report we draw on material obtained through the 16 consultative meetings, as well as on the other evidence we have received from individuals and organisations, and on the findings of studies we initiated. These studies are described briefly in the following paragraphs.

Study of arts publicity material

2.7 We started with the general impression that publicity for concerts, theatrical and film performances and other arts activities was failing to convey the information needed by disabled people who might have wished to attend. To test this, Marks and

Spencer management trainees examined for us the publicity material produced by or about arts venues in seven towns and cities in England, Wales and Scotland. The findings which, sadly, tended to confirm our belief, are summarised in Appendix 4.

Survey of access facilities at main arts venues in Edinburgh

2.8 Two volunteers, Valerie Nimmo and Teresa Wallace, conducted a survey of the 30 main arts venues in the City of Edinburgh to record physical features affecting access by disabled people, such as ramps, telephones, loop-hearing systems and adapted toilets. The survey led to continued communication between the volunteers and venues resulting in a considerable number of improvements in access facilities being made. Information gathered is now held by the recently inaugurated 'Artlink Edinburgh and the Lothians' and forms the basis of an arts information and escort service being offered to disabled and housebound people. A report is provided in Appendix 5.

Please Touch: an evaluative study of a tactile exhibition of sculpture at the British Museum

2.9 From 31 March to 8 May 1983, the British Museum held a 'Please Touch' exhibition, designed primarily for people with a visual handicap. This was the first such exhibition held at the British Museum, though there had already been a number elsewhere, including exhibitions in Ulster, Cardiff and Nottingham. The British Museum exhibits were 20 animal sculptures the oldest of which, the carving of a frog, came from Egypt and was fashioned over 5,000 years ago. In view of the lack of published guidance on the mounting of this type of exhibition and the need to encourage others to learn from the experience gained, we invited Dr Peter Coles to make an evaluation of the exhibition on our behalf. The scope of his published report is described in Appendix 6.

Guidance for funding organisations and applicants on arts projects involving disabled people

2.10 We arranged for a group under the chairmanship of Peter Cox, formerly Principal of Dartington College of Arts, to consider what guidance could be given on the assessment of arts projects affecting disabled people. The resulting publication is designed primarily to assist funding bodies wishing to finance arts projects involving disabled people. The guidelines should also be useful, however, to arts administrators and to people initiating arts projects. Three categories of funding are identified and examined - project, capital and revenue. A number of criteria are suggested for assessing projects, possible sources of advice are indicated, and the need to provide for the proper recording and evaluation of projects is emphasised. A commentary by the chairman of the group, as well as a list of the members, will be found at Appendix 7.

Arts training in Scotland: a survey of opportunities for disabled students

2.11 A study of provision for disabled students at Scottish arts colleges was undertaken by one of our members, Alexander Dunbar, formerly Director of the Scottish Arts Council. His report, summarised in Appendix 8, has already been issued, and has been used in the preparation of Chapter 9 on education and training.

'Arts for Everyone' - guidance on provision for disabled people

2.12 To fill a serious gap, we initiated the preparation of guidance notes for those running arts venues on how to make things easier for disabled people. The project was arranged in conjunction with the Centre on Environment for the Handicapped and supervised by a steering committee under the chairmanship of Hugh Spencely, chairman of the Centre. A summary of the resulting publication, and the membership of the steering committee, will be found at Appendix 9. *Arts for Everyone* will be generally available at the same time as our own report.

Archive of photographic material

2.13 We have arranged, in conjunction with the Shape/-Artlink services, for the creation of an archive of photographic material, by photographers who are themselves disabled, to illustrate the involvement of disabled people in artistic activities. The archive is to be developed and maintained by the Royal Association for Disability and Rehabilitation (RADAR), and the photographs will be used in the book which the Carnegie United Kingdom Trust has commissioned Simon Goodenough to write on matters relevant to our Inquiry.

Arts therapies

2.14 We have been conscious throughout of the important work being undertaken by qualified arts therapists in the health and social services, and to a lesser extent in education, and we established a sub-committee, with Peter Senior as convener and Sue Jennings and Daphne Kennard as members, to consider the purpose and use of arts therapy and to receive evidence. The work of this sub-committee has provided the basis for Chapter 7 which is also being made available separately with some supporting material. Arts therapists provide a valuable professional service that uses the arts as part of the whole treatment of patients in conjunction with other members of the caring professions. Any other artist, or arts instructor who works with disabled people, performs a function complementary to, rather than competitive with, the work of the professional arts therapist.

Other activities

2.15 In addition to the activities already mentioned we have made written representations on a number of public issues within our field of interest - including the effect on arts funding of the proposed abolition of the Greater London Council and the Metropolitan County Councils; the role of the newly established Access Committee for England; and proposals for changing the building regulations with a view to improving access for disabled people. We have had the advantage of a meeting with the Parliamentary All-Party Disablement Group. Our staff have been active in writing articles, giving talks, arranging exhibitions, initiating meetings on arts activities for disabled people and, insofar as time allowed, in giving guidance to individuals and organisations who approached the committee for help with their problems. In addition, our staff have taken the initiative themselves in many cases in drawing the attention of the bodies concerned to the need to cater for disabled people in new arts developments and to provide for arts facilities in new hospitals.

Chapter 3

Arts practice and provision: the present scene

3.1 Throughout this report there are references to opportunities being opened up for disabled people to become involved in the arts. To set the scene, however, we have assembled in this chapter some examples of work that is going on. All the projects and initiatives mentioned are worthwhile, and some are of outstanding merit, but we have no wish to imply that each is the best in its particular field. Nor have we sought to evaluate the importance of the contributions made by individual artists and innovators. Indeed we have tried to avoid mentioning names except where this has proved the easiest way of identifying a particular project or activity. Our comments in this chapter pave the way for recommendations made later in the report.

Scale of arts activities

3.2 The whole artistic life of the community provides the context for our Inquiry. The pervasive influence of the arts, in their many forms, cannot be defined in statistical terms but figures can be used to illustrate the scale of operations.

3.3 In the financial year 1982/83, dance, drama and opera performances in England, subsidised by the Arts Council, attracted over nine million attendances.[1] In the course of a year, about a quarter of the adult population of these islands go at least once to the theatre, opera or ballet. In London, the Royal Festival Hall attracts 20,000 concert-goers a week. Almost half a million people in England are members of amateur dramatic and operatic societies. Nearly one in ten of the population go to museums and galleries. Book issues from libraries number over 600 million a year. Twelve million books on arts and crafts subjects are sold every year. About four million adults regularly draw, paint or do craft work.[2]

3.4 Even if it were practicable, we would see no purpose in estimating how many of these people now involved in arts activities have some form of physical or mental disablement. Disabled people engaged in arts activities open to everyone should not be thought of as falling into a separate category all of their own.

Arrangement of chapter

3.5 For convenience, we have arranged this chapter so as to deal first with arts opportunities and activities for disabled people living in the community. We then go on to deal with arrangements designed specially for disabled people who live, or spend much of their time, in hospitals or other institutions.

Disabled People Living in the Community

Disabled people as performers

3.6 Recent years have seen some increase in the number of disabled people who are actors. Sometimes they act alongside non-handicapped performers and sometimes in companies of their own.

3.7 In London's West End, 'Children of a Lesser God' has played to packed houses with a profoundly deaf actress as the non-speaking deaf heroine. Though this was an American production, famous before it arrived here, the casting of a deaf actress to play a deaf part has been a notable step in the right direction for the West End stage. Earlier steps had been taken in 1974 when deaf actors were admitted as members of Equity, the actors' union.

3.8 We are glad to note that Equity is now compiling a list of actors who have a disability so that they may be particularly considered for special parts. There is an evident need for this. In one recent West End success 'Crystal Clear', sighted performers cast to play two blind characters had to be made 'blind' by being fitted with opaque contact lenses to wear on stage. Although it is far from being the case that actors who are disabled should be considered only for parts in which the character has a similar disablement, it is a reasonable presumption that in such parts they would do better than an able-bodied actor of comparable general acting ability.

Deaf people and the theatre

3.9 The problems faced by deaf people are all too little recognised, and it is worthwhile at this point to relate some of the main events in the long struggle to establish in this country professional theatre of and for the deaf. In 1961, under the auspices of the Royal National Institute for the Deaf (RNID), a mime group of 10 deaf actors was formed to provide material for the BBC programmes for deaf children. This group developed into the British Theatre of the Deaf, a full-scale company exploring many theatrical forms including dance, music, mime and sign-mime - which is a heightened and expanded version of the sign language.[3] Many performances were mounted in

13

London and elsewhere on a semi-professional basis, but it was not until 1974 that the Arts Council awarded its first grant, and the first fully professional tour was set up, with deaf actors in the majority. Recognition was given by Equity, and 12 deaf actors became provisional members.

3.10 Professional work continued on a seasonal basis, and special Associate of the Drama Board (ADB) courses were started.[4] An annual summer school, established in 1970, enabled the company to extend its influence and recruit new members. Former students from the ADB courses taught in these summer schools. In 1976, the company launched a 'theatre in education' project and went into schools for the deaf for the first time.

3.11 In 1978 two former members of the British Theatre of the Deaf founded the Interim Theatre Company, an integrated group of deaf and hearing actors. Following the policy of integrating deaf and hearing audiences, the company has presented its own version of some well-known plays, such as 'Equus' and 'A Servant of Two Masters', and has also commissioned new work. The style remains very visual, incorporating much movement, but with increasing reliance on dialogue; the actors use a form of 'signed English' to accompany the speech, which can also be lip-read by deaf people sitting in the front of the auditorium.

3.12 In 1984 the Interim Theatre Company lost its Arts Council grant but we trust that this will not be the end of all the striving which led towards professional status. A new 'theatre in education' scheme is taking projects into schools and units for the deaf and partially hearing, and the annual summer school continues.

3.13 A National Youth Theatre of the Deaf has arisen out of the work of the '66 Club', a deaf/-hearing young people's club. Under the direction of a deaf graduate of the ADB Scheme, the '66 Club Drama Section' has mounted successful productions of the popular musicals, 'The Boy Friend' and 'West Side Story'. Like those of Interim, these productions provide a notable illustration of the extent to which performances by deaf people can be enjoyed by hearing people, whether or not they understand sign language, which indeed is being developed into an artistic form in its own right.

3.14 A further wave of major activity is emerging with the systematic examination and documentation of the British Sign Language (BSL). This is quite different from 'signed English'. It is a language in its own right with its own structure, which relies not on words but on communication in terms of pictures and concepts. It is used by the majority of pre-lingually deaf people in the British Isles for communicating among themselves. Relying on BSL, a group working in conjunction with the British Deaf Association is developing a 'deaf culture'; this sets out to have its own independent roots and identity, based on the life experience of profoundly deaf people, rather than to be an adapted version of mainstream 'hearing culture'.

Other companies which include actors who are disabled

3.15 There are a number of other companies in which disabled and able-bodied actors appear together. Path Productions was launched in 1981 with a spectacular musical version of Hans Christian Anderson's fairytale, 'The Tinder Box', involving a fifty-member cast, half of whom were mentally or physically disabled. The most recent production was Shakespeare's 'A Midsummer Night's Dream', and among earlier productions had been a double bill comprising two medieval plays from China. These productions have been found to generate a warmly co-operative atmosphere in the audience, as well as in the company, and conventional audience attitudes to disabled people, including those who are mentally handicapped, are being successfully challenged. There is at present in rehearsal a production of Charles Dickens' 'A Christmas Carol' with a cast of more than 50.

3.16 Amici is a group of blind and sighted dancers. In 1983 they were joined by 15 mentally handicapped students from the Strathcona Social Education Centre, Wembley, for an enthusiastically received production of 'Ruckblick' at the Young Vic.

3.17 Probably the best-known theatre company of disabled performers is Graeae, a professional group of disabled actors and actresses whose performances in London theatres and elsewhere have been much praised in the national press. In autumn 1983 Graeae toured India with 'Casting Out', a specially commissioned script drawing on the personal experiences of company members and dramatising the problems they had had to overcome in realising their potential as actors. Audiences in Bombay, Calcutta and Delhi ranged from a group of 860 school children to members of the Indian Government, including the then Prime Minister, the late Mrs Indira Gandhi.

3.18 Graeae has also performed in the Edinburgh Fringe Festival. The company work regularly in schools, and hold workshops in colleges and institutions, so as to help other disabled people to set up acting groups and able-bodied

The Strathcona Theatre, a company of young people who are mentally handicapped, in rehearsal at their Social Education Centre, Wembley.

A scene from Rückblick

people to gain a fuller understanding of disability.

3.19 There will probably always be a place for companies such as Interim, Path, Amici and Graeae, with their special experience and knowledge of disablement. But we hope that an increasing number of disabled actors will find their way into mainstream companies, and that, in planning their repertoire, such companies will give consideration to the special needs of disabled people in their audience.

3.20 Companies which employ a high proportion of disabled performers are exploring new areas of artistic experience - both for actors and audiences - and therefore need time and scope for experimentation, which should be taken into account by funding agencies. Companies of disabled actors also have to bear extra costs, because they have to do most of their own training. There is an urgent need for full-time training for disabled students in the performing arts, as there is also for revenue grants, as opposed to project grants, because disabled actors need yearly contracts - it is particularly difficult for them if they have to be laid off intermittently.

Disabled people back-stage

3.21 There is a place for disabled people back-stage as well as out in front. In many cases, their disability will be found to have no relevance to their back-stage responsibilities, and in other cases any problems can be overcome with thought and consideration - as has been demonstrated, for example, in the case of a severely deaf girl who successfully stage-manages the work of hearing companies.

Puppetry

3.22 There is a growing recognition of the power of puppetry to delight and stimulate people of all ages, and there are a number of companies which specialise in working with disabled children.

3.23 As well as mounting theatrical productions for general audiences of school children, the Polka Puppet Theatre in Wimbledon runs classes specifically for disabled children in a well-equipped workshop with expert tuition and a high ratio of adult helpers. In a preparatory visit to their school, the puppet-maker meets the children, learns of their individual needs and assesses their capacities so that the workshop sessions can be of maximum benefit. However handicapped they may be, the children are enabled to take part in making puppets and giving performances.

3.24 The Little Angel Marionette Theatre teaches puppetry to teachers and therapists working with handicapped people. The Puppet Centre runs courses and workshops, and advises on the suitability of companies and individual puppeteers for audiences of all types. The Children's Aid Team, which runs a support service for mentally handicapped children and their families, has found that, by talking through puppets, children barely able to string two words together have suddenly been able to make themselves understood.

Creative play

3.25 Creative play is at the heart of the developing abilities of the handicapped child. The Pre-school Playgroups Associations encourage children with disabilities to become integrated with other children through their 'Open Door Opportunities Group'. Special play facilities for handicapped children are provided by the Handicapped Adventure Playground Association with many creative activities at the Linn Park Adventure Playground in Glasgow. At Hayward Playground in Islington there is a newly equipped Sound Playground for disabled children. Instruments respond to slight touch or a stroke with a soft mallet and are brightly coloured. Mentally handicapped children are found to concentrate for long periods on drawing sound from these instruments, often in co-operation with other children.

Visual arts

3.26 Disabled people working on their own, or in groups, continue to find ways of overcoming seemingly impossible odds in practising the visual arts. Of very many examples, we give three:- Carolyn James gradually lost her sight as she grew up but is achieving increasing recognition as a watercolour painter; Billy Campbell suffers from cerebral palsy but paints in oils with the help of a helmet onto which his paintbrushes are attached. Sometimes discovery of a talent in the arts opens up a new and fulfilling field of endeavour to individuals disabled in adult life - Jim Laird, confined to a wheelchair through injury as a young man, has found in sculpture an absorbing and challenging pursuit. One of his sculptures, commissioned by Stoke Mandeville where he spent some time in rehabilitation, now stands in the foyer of its Sports Centre for the Disabled.

3.27 Conquest, a society for art for the physically handicapped, regularly arranges exhibitions of the work of its members. Founded in 1978, the society co-ordinates local groups and individuals who practise the visual arts and encourages the setting up of new groups. The work of people who are mentally handicapped is displayed at annual art exhibitions mounted

Hayward Adventure Playground in London with sound sculptures for children with disabilities, created as part of an 'Interlink' project.

18

by MENCAP. There has been keen bidding to purchase some of the exhibits.

3.28 The War Pensioners' National Homecraft and Art Exhibition is held every year and includes rugs and tapestries, jewellery and leatherwork, as well as paintings, photographs and sculpture. Other arts and disability organisations such as the SCD Committee on Arts for Scotland and Project Ability in Glasgow, have mounted large, multi-media exhibitions of art and craft work by individuals with disabilities.

3.29 By the use of volunteer assistants, the Chest, Heart and Stroke Association introduces people who have had strokes to a variety of arts activities including painting, weaving and embroidery. This provides not only an absorbing interest but a means of relearning motor skills.

Art activity by a member of Conquest.

Epsom Herald, 18 February 1983

3.30 Photography for the Disabled was formed in 1968 'to encourage mentally and physically handicapped people to take up photography as a recreational hobby'. This organisation, which receives enquiries from all over the world about its work, holds an annual exhibition at which a number of trophies are awarded.

Authorship

3.31 Disablement may be no handicap to an author, but many disabled people who would like to develop their literary skills find it difficult to establish contact with other writers for purposes of mutual criticism and encouragement. With persistence, some of these people will find local writers' circles or poetry clubs they can join. Others may prefer, in the first instance, to share their work and experiences with other disabled writers, and then move on into open writers' workshops as their confidence grows. Various organisations for disabled people, such as the Spastics Society, hold literary competitions annually to give writers with disabilities an opportunity of trying out their talents in a limited field before deciding whether to take their chance in open competitions. In Oxfordshire and Berkshire a writer-in-residence, provided through Artlink/Shape and funded by the Arts Council, is available to help disabled authors.

19

3.32 Writing can be an absorbing occupation for many people who have no real prospect of seeing their work published as a commercial proposition. Positive efforts to reach isolated disabled people and encourage them to join groups and classes can be of great value. The Morley College of Adult Education provides courses specifically for writers with disabilities, the tutor himself often being someone who is disabled.

Calligraphy

3.33 The art of calligraphy is renewing its popularity. The Arts Centre run by the Gloucestershire Association for the Disabled has found so much interest in calligraphy that it is proposing to offer an 'O' level course.

Crafts

3.34 In recent years there has been a resurgence of interest in the crafts both as a hobby and as a profession. In 1971 the Government set up the Crafts Advisory Committee, now known as the Crafts Council, to encourage fine craftsmanship and to promote public interest in the work of craftsmen. This has proved a valuable initiative for the commercial development of crafts. The Council's work is limited to England but similar work has been undertaken by the Development Agencies for Northern Ireland, Scotland and Wales.

3.35 Craftwork is not only a means of occupational therapy but has also been developed as a marketable skill in sheltered workshops. A number of disability organisations such as MENCAP and the Queen Elizabeth Foundation for the Disabled have developed workshops producing goods of a very high quality in a range of crafts which include weaving, wood-carving, marquetry, leatherwork, macramé and glass engraving; and the Langhill Village Trust, for example, has had its work exhibited at the Design Centre.

3.36 In Staffordshire, the Potteries Project for the over 60s discovered numerous elderly and housebound people who were doing craftwork at home but lacked the means to market their work and had no contact with other craftsmen. A retired headmaster now organises regular exhibitions at which members' work is sold, and talks and demonstrations are given. Transport, where necessary, is provided by the Rotary Club, and the local authority hall is used at a modest rent.

3.37 The Disabled Living Foundation and the Hand Crafts Advisory Association for the Disabled are just two of the organisations that can provide help and advice in adapting techniques or on teaching methods. But despite a number of encouraging developments, there is still a need for more disabled people to be given the chance to learn craft skills and, where the prospects justify this, to set up their own businesses. Equipment of a studio at a disabled person's own home has a number of advantages, including a reduction of transport problems.

Music

3.38 It is encouraging to see, and hear, how opportunities are gradually being opened up, both amateur and professional, for musicians who are disabled. Special schools' music festivals are developing rapidly. Some special schools are inviting other nearby schools to join in, while some are holding their festivals in comprehensive schools so as to ensure a wider interest in their activities. In the Midlands and in Eastern England, the Firebird Trust (an independent body resulting from the educational programmes developed by the English Sinfonia Orchestra over the past five years) aims to benefit the community, and especially disabled people, through music and other arts. Freedom Fighter is a group of musicians in Bournemouth who write, perform and record their own songs which usually have a message about disability; four of the five musicians in the group are physically handicapped. The Northampton Footlights Group is an amateur operatic company whose disabled and able-bodied members give performances of light opera every year.

3.39 In 1983 the Adult Training Centre students attending creative music classes at the 'City Lit' in London were pleased to create and perform the background music for a film on sport and physical recreation for mentally handicapped people entitled 'Give Us the Chance'. Since then the formation of the Special Jam Band has provided many opportunities for public performance.

3.40 Music by hearing-impaired people may seem to some an unlikely combination, but a recent course, 'Music for Hearing Impaired Young People', served to demonstrate the musical ability of 37 children and young people with profound hearing losses.[5] Currently, three deaf music students are enjoying the opportunity to develop their musical potential to the full at the Royal Academy of Music, at Wadham College, Oxford and at the Dartington College of Arts. At the top professional level, Jeffrey Tate, born with spina bifida and extreme curvature of the spine, has recently been appointed as Principal Conductor of the Royal Opera House.

3.41 An increasing amount of practical help is being made available to disabled people who want to make music. For instance, in Devon a special foundation has been established to enable music teachers to visit disabled people regularly in their own homes; while, among other aids, Rehabilitation Engineering

Movement Advisory Panels (REMAP) have designed and made:- (i) a piano pedalling device controlled by the chin for a pianist who lost the use of his legs following an accident, and (ii) an adjustable music stand for a partially-sighted harpist, which can be moved up and down by a foot control and is nearer the eyes than normal.

3.42 Training initiatives in different parts of the country bringing together people in the various disciplines concerned with music and disabled people are providing opportunities for confidence building in, and encouragement for, those disabled people who might otherwise be too apprehensive to 'have a go'.

Museums, galleries and historic buildings

3.43 In the next chapter we refer briefly to some ways of making museums, galleries and historic buildings more accessible to disabled people. A fuller account, the first systematic guidance to be published in this country, is given in 'Arts for Everyone', which we ourselves commissioned, as explained in Chapter 2.12 and Appendix 9.

3.44 Many museums and similar establishments have tried to provide improved physical access for disabled people, but there is a growing recognition that this is by no means enough. One evident need is to do much more

to enable disabled people to gain advantage from the range of events, such as special exhibitions and activity programmes, which go beyond traditional methods of presentation and are increasingly being used to bring collections to life so as to appeal to a wider audience.

3.45 There have been some encouraging signs. The Education Service of the Glasgow Museums and Galleries has a well-developed programme for mentally handicapped children. Often started with the needs of visually handicapped visitors in mind, tactile exhibitions and discovery rooms are rapidly developing into a new mode of experiencing museum exhibits for everyone. A tactile exhibition of contemporary sculpture is currently being presented at the Castle Museum, Nottingham in conjunction with the Arts Council of Great Britain. Every month in the British Museum there is a gallery talk which is interpreted in sign language for the benefit of visitors with impaired hearing. Museums are also bringing their collections to a wider public by means of travelling exhibitions, and by arranging for talks in hospitals and other institutions where selected exhibits can be shown and handled.

3.46 Valuable as they are, however, such initiatives all too often depend on the enthusiasm of a few individuals, when what is needed is an integrated plan of

Gallery talk at the British Museum with sign language interpreter.

development in which all members of the staff are involved. In the result, provision for disabled people remains very patchy even within particular establishments, let alone over the country as a whole. However enlightened the general policies may be, their success ultimately depends on what is done at local level, and even the finest facilities can be rendered virtually useless in the absence of a co-operative attitude on the part of the staff. Hence the importance of staff training to which we return in Chapter 4.41.

Community arts organisations

3.47 Community arts organisations, which are usually small and committed to responding to grass-roots needs, are well placed - despite their limited resources - to help disabled people fulfil themselves through arts activities. There have already been welcome moves in the right direction. Worcester Arts Workshop, a successful community arts organisation with a well-equipped workshop, states explicitly in the information leaflet describing its new facilities that 'all this will be available for everyone including the disabled'. Theatre Workshop in Edinburgh has an excellent reputation for the welcome disabled people and groups can rely on receiving, despite access facilities which are less than ideal and despite the fact that their availability is not yet included in its publicity material.

The choice between separate and integrated arts activities for disabled people living in the community

3.48 It would be of great advantage if far more arts clubs and societies, and art galleries and art centres, made a real effort to encourage disabled people to join in. But separate arts facilities specifically for disabled people will continue to be needed. In some cases, a disabled person will be able to play a part in the arts activities of other members of the community after an initial period gaining experience in a separate setting; in some cases, the disablement may be too severe to enable the individual ever to take advantage of general facilities; and in some cases, given the choice, disabled people may prefer to follow artistic pursuits in company with others whose circumstances and difficulties are similar to their own.

3.49 The element of choice is of crucial importance. A good example is provided by the arrangements at the Royal Academy's Summer Exhibition. Assistance is available to disabled people visiting the exhibition on general public days. But, in addition, one day is set aside especially for disabled people, when extra help and facilities are provided, and the gallery is free of the usual crowds.

Classes and workshops

3.50 An increasing number of community centres, arts centres and further education colleges are developing arts courses for disabled people. Sometimes these are introductory courses in which skills can be acquired to equip the disabled person to join an open group later on. The use of community venues provides opportunities for disabled people to meet each other, to learn about outside activities, and to be drawn into community life. The growth in community psychiatric services should be accompanied by a corresponding growth in the arts facilities made available to the patients in community venues. And there is a growing need to provide elderly people with an opportunity to exercise their creative powers; the Niccol Arts Centre in Cirencester caters particularly for elderly people.

3.51 A weekly dance class for mentally handicapped people which was held at the Pineapple Dance Studios in London proved a great success. The weekly trip to Covent Garden, and the excitement of attending a dance centre, enhanced considerably the enjoyment of those taking part. Artshare South West have funded two artists to run drama activities in the local library for children from special schools. As a by-product, this arrangement has provided the children with an opportunity to establish an interest in books which they might otherwise have lacked.

3.52 The Association for Spina Bifida and Hydrocephalus (ASBH) provides accommodation and help for disabled students attending one-term non-vocational courses at Ilkley College where a wide range of arts and crafts skills are taught. For students attending the two-year residential course at Beaumont College, the Spastics Society College of Further Education, the curriculum of social, vocational and aesthetic training centres on dance, drama, music and the visual arts.

3.53 When made the subject of public presentations, arts courses involving disabled people have been found to have a value beyond their training function. Bringing the work done on such courses to public notice increases general understanding of the needs and the abilities of disabled people. One happy example comes from the residential course on visual arts run by the SCD Committee on Arts for Scotland. Through co-operation between the course organisers and one of Scottish Opera's commercial sponsors, a painting by one of the participants was used as a publicity poster for a new opera production.

Activity holidays and summer schools

3.54 Holidays and summer schools incorporating arts activities are becoming popular with disabled people. Some are subsidised through grants from charitable trusts or local authorities, while others charge

Photos by Martin Mayer of London

The magic of a theatre workshop with the Interplay Community Theatre.

fees high enough to make them self-supporting. The Winged Fellowship Trust runs a series of highly successful arts and crafts holidays in conjunction with the Highway Theatre Company; physically disabled people are given the opportunity to study in depth all aspects of theatre. Participants write the play, make costumes and scenery, and devise the music, make-up and lighting. The aim is to develop the full potential of each participant. Similar holidays including painting, photography, needlecraft and pottery are made available and the 'Music Lovers' Fortnight' includes visits to musical instrument collections and concerts.

3.55 The Royal National Institute for the Blind (RNIB) has for some years co-ordinated a drama summer school from which a number of students have gone on to classes which have mounted public performances. Based on the work of an advisory group set up by the Carnegie UK Trust, the RNIB has also been concerned with the establishment of five regional drama groups and the recent formation of the National Association of Drama with the Visually Handicapped.

Disabled People in Institutions

3.56 There are a whole variety of institutions in which disabled people live or spend much of their time. These include schools, colleges, training and rehabilitation centres, sheltered workshops, work centres and day centres, as well as hostels, residential homes, hospitals and hospices.

3.57 Under current policy the trend is towards limiting long-stay institutional care to people for whom community care would be impracticable. But for many years to come there will be a substantial number of long-stay hospitals, and there will always be some people who require long-term care in an institution. In such cases, the aim must be to provide an environment as similar as possible to that of a normal home. Arts provision can play a central part in this humanising process. Over the past 20 years there have been some significant achievements but these hardly do more than point the way. The scope for development is vast. In the following paragraphs we refer to some of the arts opportunities for disabled people living in institutions, and then go on to describe some of the agencies operating in this area.

Visual arts

3.58 For people in hospitals and other institutions to engage in drawing and painting, threadwork, embroidery or weaving, the essential minimum requirement is access to relatively inexpensive materials and pieces of simple equipment. A start in organising these activities may be made by a sympathetic person who, even without specialist knowledge or training, believes strongly enough in the enterprise to stimulate and encourage disabled people to develop their own ideas and to try to find the art materials which suit them best. But, although rudimentary arrangements and materials are better than none, progressive improvement must be the aim with the employment of whatever additional resources can be found, and involvement of the caring professions in providing

'A Sense of Movement' – Work by Veronica Sherborne

Adults give children a sense of security in different ways of containing and supporting.

the organisational framework. To operate to the best advantage, volunteers assisting in arts activities need to work within a professional framework for arts and arts therapies. In chapters 6 and 7 we make proposals for the establishment of such a framework.

3.59 In most hospitals and institutions there has hitherto been little provision for individual arts activities. But where the facilities are provided they are usually well used. A lecturer in art for the elderly with the Inner London Education Authority, has been notably successful in encouraging elderly patients to paint and draw, with excellent results. Spaces, designed as 'art studios', have been allocated in several hospitals, and in one hospital a purpose-built art studio has been provided in the grounds. Once a degree of confidence has been achieved, the enthusiastic elderly person may well have acquired an absorbing interest for life. In the history of art there are many examples of first-class work being produced at an advanced age. In some instances a lifetime devoted to art has been crowned by the achievements in old age, but in other instances talents hitherto undeveloped have been recognised for the first time in later life.

3.60 The value of such activities should not be measured primarily by outsiders' judgements of the product; the personal satisfaction and opportunities for self-expression engendered may well be of greater importance. Physical or mental limitations are soon forgotten when the will to paint is uppermost. In illustration of this, one has only to consider the achievements of artists who use their mouths or their feet to manipulate their brushes.

3.61 Photography is an activity which can become very popular among disabled people, whether or not they live in institutions. As well as tuition, however, facilities are needed for pictures to be developed and printed. At present, these facilities are rarely provided in the institutions where disabled people live.

Performing arts

3.62 Some individual performers and some companies, such as Action Space London Events, experiment with new approaches specially adapted to institutional settings. The particular needs of each audience are assessed and presentations are developed which require the active involvement of the staff and volunteers, as well as of the disabled people themselves, in creating the drama. In some cases there is a need for extensive preparation by the staff, either on the basis of guidance notes produced by the arts group or of discussion with them. Specific learning goals for the disabled people may be built into the presentation by co-operation between the arts group and the teaching, care or therapy staff. The final product is likely to draw heavily on dramatic techniques but to achieve the desired effect may also make use of a whole range of art forms, including music, dance and puppetry.

3.63 In carrying such work forward there are many difficulties of funding and facilities to be faced, but there is also a need to ensure that the activities involved do not conflict with medical treatment or requirements. Nonetheless, very promising results have been achieved in cases where the arts group has been enabled to enlist the enthusiastic support of those running the institution.

3.64 Handicapped children in Somerset and Avon benefit from drama participation and creative play workshops which the Children's World charity organises. The drama participation team visits seven special schools every week and has done so for the past seven terms. A new departure is the Children's World omnibus tour of creative play, taking arts and craft workshops and specialised play facilities regularly to more than 20 institutions in Somerset and Avon. The charity also make inflatables and custom-built wooden play equipment for special schools. Theatre Workshop, Edinburgh has one worker whose time is devoted to presenting theatre to children in institutions and providing training courses for staff.

3.65 Interplay Community Theatre, a professional theatre company based in Leeds, specialises in work in hospitals and elsewhere with people who are mentally handicapped. Over the past 10 years performances have been given for children with special needs at various schools in Yorkshire and also on visits to London and the East Midlands. Recently two short residencies have been held in Yorkshire and the East Midlands to pass on to teachers some of the company's ideas and techniques for involving children and staff in role play and informal workshops.

3.66 Carousel in Brighton uses drama and visual arts skills to lead workshops in schools, day centres and hospitals. These workshops are conducted mainly with people who are mentally handicapped, but also with others, including children and adults suffering from cerebral palsy, and with emotionally disturbed children.

3.67 Among the many manifestations of dance and movement are disco, ballet, folk dancing and wheelchair dancing. Ludus Dance Company with its project for special schools - 'The Thunder Tree' - worked with 2,500 children and workers in special education over a period of 18 months and provided teachers with training in the skills of dance and movement. The company found that the teachers felt a need for a continuing developmental programme of training in these skills. In the Royal Marsden Hospital, Surrey music and dance play a very important part in the lives of patients who are fired by the enthusiasm of the Director of Nursing Services.

3.68 Pioneering work with mentally handicapped children and their teachers has done much to convince educationalists of the value of movement activities in promoting growth and learning. Using a graded series of movement exercises that are first and foremost fun to do, severely mentally handicapped children at all stages of their development are able to learn about their bodies and how to control them, about working with others, and about sharing with others in progressively larger groups.[6]

Exhibitions held in institutions

3.69 Institutions in which disabled people spend their time can make excellent sites for arts exhibitions and the display of museum exhibits, combined in some cases with handling sessions, lectures, films or slide-shows. Such events are not only of direct value to the disabled people concerned but also have the advantage of attracting people from outside, so that those in the institution come to feel less isolated. This effect has been apparent at the RNIB College for the Blind which, as well as mounting its own exhibitions, is a receiving gallery for travelling exhibitions mounted by the Arts Council. Among the museums which have been active in similar ventures is the Leeds City Museum which has taken objects to children in long-stay wards and to psychiatric patients using day-care facilities.

3.70 A number of new hospitals have established substantial art collections of their own. At the Leicester Royal Infirmary, for instance, the enthusiasm and determination of the architects, administrators and medical staff has led to a collection of contemporary art being acquired, which local teachers bring parties to see. The new St Thomas's Hospital, London has some 600 works by over 100 artists, and is said to be the hospital with the largest collection of art in Britain. Painting in Hospitals, started in 1959 with charitable funds to provide paintings to hang in hospitals, now has over 1,350 paintings. This is one of the largest collections of contemporary paintings in this country outside government ownership. An exhibition is held annually to enable hospitals to select paintings for their own walls.

Festivals

3.71 The larger long-stay institutions often have extensive grounds which can provide a pleasant setting for arts festivals. Some years ago One-to-One were instrumental in mounting a series of one-day festivals in the grounds of mental handicap hospitals. At these events members of the local community relaxed alongside residents. Full-scale festivals take a lot of organising but an annual gala day in hospital grounds can have a lasting effect on morale and community attitudes.

Visits to outside arts events

3.72 Most people go to arts events in small groups, with their families or friends, and perhaps the happiest arrangement for people in institutions is to go accompanied by one other person. Schemes which provide one-to-one companionship for disabled people going to cultural events are very demanding on the time and energies of organisers and participants, but their benefits can be tremendous. Artlink in Edinburgh is experimenting with a volunteer scheme linked to an information service, which tests escort, transport and access facilities.

3.73 Sometimes people in institutions who wish to go out to cultural events are unable to do so because of lack of transport though they could afford to hire a taxi, or share the cost of hire with a fellow resident. Difficulties can arise, however, in using private funds for this purpose. The typical case relates to benefits and allowances held in accounts by institutions on behalf of the residents.

3.74 Medical staff and others have raised with us the question of who should be able to authorise the use of a patient's own money, and for what purposes. We recognise that this can raise difficult legal and moral issues, but it is very important that ways acceptable to disabled people should be found for authorising the use of funds of residents in long-stay hospitals and other settings. Otherwise, money will continue to accumulate over long periods which should be used to improve the quality of life for the residents concerned. We have found that there is a great deal of justified anxiety about this.

Organisations bringing arts activities and events into institutions

3.75 A number of non-profit making organisations and administrative teams have been established with a particular concern for bringing arts activities and events to disabled people in institutions. One of the most successful of these organisations is Shape which was set up in London in 1976 to serve as an agency for placing professional artists, as performers and workshop leaders, in areas of special need including hospitals, day centres and residential homes.[7]

31

3.76 From its starting point in London, the Shape concept (sometimes under the name Artlink or Artshare) has spread elsewhere in the United Kingdom by the creation of a network of 14 independent but associated services. The subsequent founding of Interlink has given the Shape idea an international dimension.

3.77 Shape is already playing a vital role but the scope and scale of its activities are sadly restricted by lack of funds, and time which might be spent on developing Shape services has perforce to be devoted to fund-raising. In addition to its more general purposes in bringing arts activities to disabled people, Shape has the specific aim of providing the expertise, support and finance needed to get particular projects through their initial stages. Lack of resources not only limits this work but can do positive harm if projects are undermined by insufficient preparation time or cannot be maintained long enough to have a fair trial.

3.78 Another type of administrative structure evolved to organise a range of arts activities is that of the arts team based in an institution. The Manchester Hospitals Arts Project is probably the most familiar and comprehensive example.

3.79 The project was initiated by the present Director following his experiences of working voluntarily as an artist and teacher in St Mary's Hospital, Manchester. In 10 years it has developed to a point where a team of 17 artists are involved together with students and volunteers. The project uses a full range of arts activities and events including textile/fibre arts, paintings, murals, photography, puppetry, music and performances of all kinds. Funding has been obtained from many different sources including the three Manchester Health Authorities, the local Education Committee, the Inner City Partnership and the Regional Arts Association. Fund-raising efforts and donations provide a considerable supplement.

3.80 Endless cream and grey painted corridors and intimidating waiting areas have been transformed with paintings, murals and humorous signposting. Patients, visitors and staff benefit from the visually relaxing environment. A playground designed for bedbound and wheelchair-bound children is just one of many examples where the sensitive imagination of artists has complemented the standard health service provision. The presence of the arts team has significantly improved the atmosphere of the hospitals, health centres and clinics which they serve.

3.81 In any District Health Authority the work of an artist or an arts team needs to be supplemented and supported by artists and performances coming in from the community to add to the richness of an arts programme. A hospital-based team can however provide the necessary focus by creating an organised framework adapted to the needs of the patients and staff of the institution concerned.

3.82 Experience in the Manchester Hospitals Arts Project suggests that an integrated programme of arts activities cannot be successfully imposed from outside, but has to evolve from within the institution or group. Unless a senior member of the medical or administrative staff gives active encouragement any project will be severely hampered. To get the best from performers and groups coming in from outside there must be careful preparation to ensure that the programme is well suited to the particular audience, and especially that there is no 'playing down' to them, and also that full account is taken of any limitations of space or technical resources. Within the institution there should be a senior member of the staff who will take personal responsibility for co-ordinating the arrangements, and for ensuring that after the performance there is a feed-back from the patients and staff so that the performers will learn more about the impact they have made and if there are any problems they can be sorted out before the next visit.

3.83 The Northgate Hospital Arts Project provides an example of a less widely-based arrangement than that operating in Manchester. In 1982 the 700-bedded Northgate Hospital in Northumberland - a long-stay hospital for mentally handicapped people - employed a co-ordinator to set up and run a wide range of creative activities. This was the first such project in the northern region and as such focused attention on the lack of existing provision. The project has attracted a wide range of artists who, anxious to work in this field, would otherwise have lacked the guidance and support that the project teams provide.

Isle of Wight Health Authority

3.84 The Pioneering work of artists and administrators in various health authorities led the architects of the DHSS Directorate of Development to commission a report on 'Art in the NHS'[8] from the author of *The Manchester Hospitals Arts Project*.[9] The same author and the Director of the Manchester Hospitals Arts Project have been acting as consultants in the planning of the new St Mary's General Hospital.[10] The object has been to ensure from the outset that appropriate provision for the arts is incorporated into the design of the hospital and that consideration is given to an arts programme for the whole of the District Health Authority. Research showed that providing programmes and facilities for disabled people and those in community care would require arts venues around the island to be made more accessible. The local authorities and arts funding bodies are co-operating in this to plan for the future. A group of volunteers under the chairmanship of the County Music Adviser is assisting.

Arrangements for musical performances in hospitals

3.85 As our final example of a useful administrative innovation, we wish to refer to arrangements made for facilitating musical performances in hospitals. Many of the difficulties involved can be alleviated if a body with experience in this area assumes general responsibility for matters of administration and finance, leaving the artists to concentrate on their own performances. This function is served by the Council for Music in Hospitals which now puts on about a thousand concerts a year. On a smaller scale, Live Music Now also operates in this field by arranging some of its concerts in hospitals and other venues where many of those attending are handicapped. As we have already indicated, the arrangements will work best if such organisations have a liaison officer within the hospital with whom to collaborate.

3.86 The two organisations we have mentioned provide for artists to be auditioned, fees to be paid (by combining a contribution from the receiving venue with funds provided by charitable donations) and administrative arrangements to be looked after. Both organisations run training days for their musicians; and performances are followed up so that constructive criticism can be offered. The interest of potential future performers is engaged through a short course which the Royal Academy of Music runs for its students in conjunction with the Council for Music in Hospitals.

3.87 A new development is a course for fourth-year students at the Guildhall School of Music and Drama. As part of the course, performances will be given at unorthodox venues. The aim is 'to eliminate the capital C in culture', and to allow students to extend their learning experience by performing in front of widely differing audiences.

3.88 In these and other ways, the arrangements for musical performances in institutions are in advance of those for other arts events. The Music Adviser to the Disabled Living Foundation is, to our knowledge, the only full-time officer employed in a national disability organisation to gather and disseminate information and advice about a particular art form.

General

3.89 Although this account of current developments is by no means exhaustive we should be wrong to leave the impression that the effort matches the need.

This is very far from being the case. Plans should be developed on an altogether larger scale for encouraging disabled people to participate in arts activities, and should allow full scope for disabled people themselves to make their wishes known and to help in making them effective. What in many places is now a mere trickle should become a flood. In the remainder of our report we suggest some ways in which the urgent needs of the situation can begin to be more adequately met.

References

1 Arts Council of Great Britain.
Bulletin No 66, ACGB, London, April 1984
(Note also 'Facts and Figures' issued annually by ACGB, Information Department, London.)

2 Central Council of Amateur Theatre.
Amateur Theatre in Great Britain, CCAT, London, 1979

3 Keysell, Pat.
Motives for Mime, Evans Bros, London, 1975

4 The Drama Board was formed in 1949 and closed in 1981 when responsibility for its ADB qualification was transferred to the Royal Society of Arts, John Adam Street, London. A special course with a qualification for deaf students is organised by Bulmershe College, Reading.

5 Disabled Living Foundation.
Resource papers - Music Advisory Service, DLF, London

6 Kirby, Margaret.
Sherborne and Movement, Bristol Polytechnic, 1984
(Note: The film 'A Sense of Movement' by Veronica Sherborne, 1976 is available from Concord Films Council, Ipswich.)

7 Levete, Gina.
No Handicap to Dance, Human Horizons Series of Souvenir Press, London, 1982

8 Coles, Peter.
Art in the National Health Service, DHSS, London, 1983

9 Coles, Peter.
The Manchester Hospitals Arts Project, Calouste Gulbenkian Foundation, London, 1981

10 Department of Health and Social Security.
Isle of Wight Health Authority Arts Provision, DHSS, London, 1985

Note: The details and addresses of organisations mentioned in this and other chapters are available from the Music Adviser, Disabled Living Foundation, 380-384 Harrow Road, London W9 2HU. See also Appendix 2.

Chapter 4

Information and accessibility

4.1 In this chapter we discuss various ways of making the arts more accessible to disabled people. This involves not only securing easier physical access to arts buildings, but also tackling other obstacles which preclude disabled people from sharing fully in the arts opportunities open to their fellow citizens. Among the matters to be considered are the adaptation of facilities within buildings, the training of staff, the provision of adequate information and the arrangements for transport to and from arts venues.

4.2 There are three preliminary points to be made. First, attitudes can be more important than physical provision so the most valuable measures are not necessarily the most costly - the proper training of staff, for instance, can be even more important than structural alterations to buildings. Second, more effective dissemination of information is often the single greatest need - because unless people can get to know about them, it matters little how good the facilities are. Third,

developments introduced to help disabled people are often of advantage to others also. It is not only people with walking difficulties or poor sight who benefit from non-slip floor coverings, uncluttered corridors, adequate lighting and well-sited direction signs. It is not only people with impaired hearing who benefit from clear and deliberate speech by performers, lecturers and guides.

Access Committees

4.3 Committees charged with considering the general access problems of disabled people on a national basis have now been appointed for each country of the United Kingdom. The most recently established is the Access Committee for England. This was set up in 1983, on government initiative and with government funding, and is being serviced by the Centre on Environment for the Handicapped.[1] The Committee is intended to give advice and support to local access groups; advise local authorities who are considering the designation of access officers; consider access problems of national relevance, including the implications of legislation; promote public awareness of access problems; and provide a focal point on access matters for individual disabled people, referring enquirers as appropriate to relevant organisations.

4.4 The Access Committees for Scotland, Wales and Northern

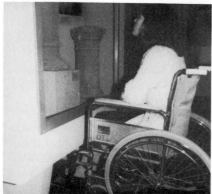

2 3

Three examples of useful improvements in museuems:
1. Ramped entrance to a side gallery; the Egyptian Sculpture gallery at the British Museum.
2. Handrails to assist the walking disabled visitor at the Victoria and Albert Museum.
3. Creation of space to permit close examination of an exhibit by a visitor in a wheelchair at the Devizes Museum.

Ireland have been in operation for a longer period, with objectives similar to those of the English committee. In Scotland, the Accessibility Panel of the Scottish Council on Disability (SCD) became the Scottish Committee on Access for Disabled People in 1980, and since June 1984 has been called the SCD Committee on Access for Scotland. Its activities have included offering advice on legislation; encouraging local access panels and access officers; promoting conferences, seminars and training courses; and, in 1981, publishing an *Access for Disabled People Handbook*.[2] The committee continues to be active in these areas, and in working with the Scottish Tourist Board to provide access to all categories of tourist accommodation and to leisure and recreational facilities. There is not yet, however, any plan for providing a comprehensive list of the access facilities at arts venues in Scotland.

4.5 Many of the points we make in this chapter come within the remits of the national Access Committees, and we hope that they will find our comments and recommendations helpful in developing their own policies.

Building regulations

4.6 In 1983 the Department of the Environment issued consultative papers on the introduction of a new building regulation for England and Wales, dealing with access and facilities for disabled people in buildings open to the public. In the light of reactions to the initial draft, the Department issued a revised draft regulation under which, when a building for public use was being erected or altered, means of access for disabled people would have to be provided, but only to the ground floor. It was intended that the requirement should be extended to all floors when the British Standards Institution had completed a British Standard covering the evacuation of disabled people from buildings in an emergency. Wheelchair spaces were to be provided in auditoria, to the extent of at least eight or, if less, 0.5 per cent of the number of seats; and where toilets were provided, a reasonable number were to be accessible to, and designed to meet the needs of, disabled people.

4.7 In commenting on the draft regulation, we expressed our concern to the Department about any limitation of the proposed requirements to the ground floor alone. We urged that nothing should be done which could give currency to the idea that in buildings used for arts activities, such as libraries, museums and galleries, theatres and arts centres, it would be sufficient to concentrate on the main entrance floor so far as the needs of disabled people were concerned. We made the further points that (a) the proposed scale of provision for wheelchairs was inadequate; (b) in the design and alteration of buildings for use by the public, proper consideration should be given to the means of installing systems enabling people with impaired hearing to participate in events; and (c) even though the regulation did not apply to Crown property, the requirements should in practice be as rigorously applied there as elsewhere.

4.8 In September 1984, after consulting the Parliamentary All-Party Disablement Group, the Department of the Environment invited comments on proposals which had been further revised. Under these proposals, access was to be provided to and within all new single-storey structures to which the public have access. For halls and auditoria the formula for the minimum provision of wheelchair spaces was to be six, or a number in excess of 1/100th of the total number of seats available to the public, whichever was the greater. In buildings within the scope of the regulations, if sanitary conveniences were provided, a reasonable number (at least one) were to be accessible to, and designed for use by, disabled people. Regulations requiring the provision of access for disabled people to all floors of all new buildings were to be introduced as soon as possible after the British Standards Institute had developed authoritative guidance on means of escape for disabled people from such buildings.[3]

4.9 In commenting on these new proposals, we deplored the limitation to new single-storey buildings, which would mean that the majority of arts buildings were excluded. Among our other comments was a recommendation that the regulations should cover alterations and extensions, as previously proposed. An increasing number of arts buildings are adapted from existing buildings such as warehouses and churches.

4.10 In Northern Ireland a new regulation has already been made, based on access to the ground floor only, taking effect from 1 December 1984.[4] In Scotland a similar regulation takes effect from 4 March 1985.[5]

4.11 We are very concerned that swifter progress has not been made towards providing disabled people with full access to arts venues. Existing technical solutions to means of escape problems may well require greater codification, but we are not satisfied that the solutions themselves are inadequate. We *recommend* that, without further delay, building regulations should require that access be provided for disabled people to and within all floors of arts buildings to which members of the public may be admitted; and that there should be a reasonable number of toilets designed to meet the needs of disabled people, which they can reach easily from any part of the building. The provisions must be such as to meet the needs of disabled employees as well as the needs of visitors, and should be applicable throughout the United Kingdom. They should apply to major alterations and extensions as well as to new buildings.

Conditions of licensing

4.12 Access by disabled people to existing public buildings depends not only on physical possibilities but also on the licensing conditions laid down on the advice of fire officers. We have heard a great many complaints about the operation of the licensing system. It is contended that unrealistic assumptions are made - not adequately based on either experience or research - about the dangers of exits being blocked by wheelchairs; that insufficient attention is given to the scope for minimising any danger by efficient management procedures; and that the conditions laid down vary arbitrarily from place to place, and from one time to another. The needs of disabled performers have caused particular difficulties. We have heard of one new arts building where the stage entrances were deliberately made wide enough for wheelchairs, but had to be made narrower again so as actually to preclude wheelchair entry before the fire officer would approve the building as safe. In other instances, approval has been given by a fire officer, only to be rescinded shortly afterwards for no convincing reason. To avoid this, it was suggested to us at some of our consultative meetings that, other than in the most exceptional circumstances, approval once given for a particular set of arrangements should last for a specified minimum period.

4.13 In the light of the comments we have received, we are convinced that there should now be a thorough reappraisal of the way in which the safety legislation is working. There is a need to establish, in the light of research, the nature and extent of any special risk arising from the presence of disabled people in public buildings. We therefore *recommend* that (a) the Home Secretary (in consultation with the Secretary of State for the Environment, and the Secretaries of State for Northern Ireland, Scotland and Wales) should arrange for a review of the operation of the legislation relating to the licensing of buildings for use by the public; (b) this review, which should sponsor any necessary research, should be conducted with the help of organisations for disabled people, and should involve planners, architects, and designers, as well as fire officers and venue managers; and (c) two of the main objects should be to provide fire officers with clearer and more detailed directions and guidance, and to devise a national code of practice, based on a presumption of access, which would promote positive attitudes towards disabled people amongst those who administer licences and the managers of arts venues.

Arts for Everyone

4.14 We have already referred to the arrangements we have made, in conjunction with the Centre on Environment for the Handicapped, for the preparation of guidance notes, under the title *Arts for Everyone*, on how to make things easier for disabled people at arts venues. These notes will be the first comprehensive guide for arts administrators on this subject, and will take into account the various matters we discuss below.

Adaptation of buildings and their main furnishings

4.15 It will be many years before the full benefits accrue from taking the needs of disabled people into account when buildings are being constructed or altered. In the meantime, a great deal will depend on the efforts made to adapt existing buildings. In some cases ramped entrances for wheelchairs, and lifts between floors, will be needed, with better car-parking facilities. But other, less expensive, developments can also be valuable. Many people with walking disabilities can negotiate steps if a simple handrail is

A sensible and successful attempt to provide access by ramp and bell-push to an old building used as an Arts Centre.

erected. Through advances in technology, portable stair-climbers can now be purchased relatively cheaply and, in some buildings, no installation work is needed before they are brought into use. Adapted toilets are important, but so are details like telephone height, non-slip surfaces, and the placing of upright seats at key points so that disabled people can take a rest.

4.16 In theatres and other buildings with an auditorium, it is a great help to have some seats which can be removed and replaced by wheelchairs as occasion requires. This is a flexible arrangement of benefit to management and wheelchair users alike. One of the advantages for wheelchair users is that they are enabled to sit with their friends among the rest of the audience. In museums and galleries the height of the show-cases and the angle at which they are set will largely determine how much of the contents can be seen from a wheelchair. In libraries, the bookshelves should be set far enough apart for a person in a wheelchair to be able to move between them.

4.17 In some cases the cost of the adaptations will be beyond the means of those responsible for the buildings. To enable progress to be made, we *recommend* that the Minister for the Arts should make funds available for adapting arts venues to make them more accessible to disabled people. One way of doing this would be to introduce an incentive scheme modelled on the new Business Sponsorship Incentive Scheme (BSIS) but with a broader base. The BSIS is administered by the Association for Business Sponsorship for the Arts (ABSA) on behalf of the Office of Arts and Libraries.[6] The scheme provides for the 'topping up' of sponsorship money, from business firms only, with a minimum payment from the firm of £7,500. The funds we propose for adaptations would need to be available to 'top up' payments from local authorities or any other source, and the qualifying minimum payment would need to be much less than £7,500. Many arts venues - including historic buildings, leisure centres and some museums - are outside the responsibility of the Minister for the Arts. We *recommend* that the Minister for the Disabled should co-ordinate arrangements for funds to be made available to help with adaptations in such cases.

4.18 Uniform arrangements should apply throughout the United Kingdom, and we *recommend* therefore that the Secretary of State for Northern Ireland should introduce arrangements in Northern Ireland corresponding to those in Great Britain.

People with impaired vision

4.19 In all arts venues, people who are virtually blind, or whose sight is poor, will gain great benefit from easy-to-read direction signs, from an effective lighting system, from marked edges to steps, from raised numbers on lift buttons, from agreed arrangements for accepting guide-dogs, and from being enabled to sit in front rows at concert halls and theatres.

4.20 In museums and galleries, labels may be too small for any but the most sharp-sighted to distinguish, and increasingly tend to be produced in low-contrast colours which are hard to make out, or are at an inconvenient height for able-bodied and disabled people alike. There are some sensitive objects which would deteriorate in strong light, but even where such considerations do not apply there is often subtle lighting in display cases which has been conceived as part of the total design. This may mean that people with poor vision

Interpretative display with clear presentation at the Captain Cook Birthplace Museum.

Blind people and others can enjoy a tactile exhibition

42

cannot see the exhibits well, or even at all. Yet a balance in lighting could be achieved, keeping people with impaired vision in mind, without destroying the designers' intentions by flooding everything with bright light.

4.21 Guide books and catalogues are rarely well-adapted for use by people whose sight is poor; and such people can benefit considerably from being able to listen to information on cassette about particular exhibitions and about arts facilities generally. The same applies to theatre and music programmes.

4.22 Where this is consistent with proper regard for the preservation and safety of the exhibits in museums and historic houses, the opportunity to touch the exhibits will be appreciated not only by people with impaired vision but by many other people

also. In paragraph 2.9 we have referred to the 'Please Touch' exhibition held in the British Museum, and to some of the similar exhibitions held previously elsewhere.

4.23 In some museums objects which may be touched are placed together in a designated area and changed every now and again. This facility is likely to attract many visitors besides people with impaired vision and can be of particular advantage to visitors for whom a tour of the exhibition halls poses problems.

4.24 Education staff in museums can involve groups with special needs in handling sessions, during which the background to, and special significance of, particular objects can be explained and explored.

People with impaired hearing

4.25 Deafness is one of the most common forms of disablement, and yet attracts perhaps the least public understanding. Deaf people can sometimes encounter such a lack of sympathy for their problems as to make it seem that they were suspected of feigning deafness.

4.26 In important respects, the needs of people who are profoundly deaf differ from those of people with a lesser degree of hearing loss. But both groups come within the scope of the Sympathetic Hearing Scheme,

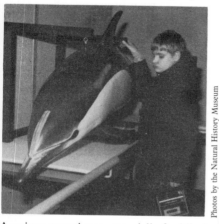

Photos by the Natural History Museum

A unique experience, especially for blind children – exploring woodland and seashore at the Natural History Museum with a taped commentary and braille captions . . . and touch.

which is administered and financed by four major charities for the deaf, with support from the Government. At arts venues displaying the symbol of the Sympathetic Hearing Scheme, a stylised ear shape, someone should be available who will take trouble to communicate with deaf people, even though there may be no-one who knows sign-language. Anyone who has difficulty in hearing can obtain a plastic card with the Sympathetic Hearing Scheme symbol on it, and can produce the card when they need help.

4.27 Staff at arts venues can readily be given simple advice on ways of helping deaf people - by, for example, taking care to articulate clearly and facing towards the light. It is still better if a member of the staff is prepared to spend time learning even a smattering of sign language and to be on call as necessary. Virtually every city and town has a Club for the Deaf and it would not be difficult to find a social worker or some other willing person who could give the necessary instruction. In some arts venues it should be possible to go well beyond this and use signing interpreters on certain occasions - for example, at one theatre performance a week, or regularly at museum and gallery lectures.

4.28 Since 1974 over 1½ million hearing aids have been issued by the National Health Service, all capable of receiving audio-frequency induction loop transmissions. The installation of induction loop systems, which eliminate all extraneous 'audience noise', can make an enormous difference to those who wear this type of hearing aid and switch it to the 'T' position. Infra-red systems give even better reproduction, but although the listener does not need to have a hearing aid he has to borrow or hire a special head-set; and both the system itself and the head-set are more expensive. The general adoption of one or other of these two systems could transform the lives of some deaf people.

4.29 It would be a further step forward if theatre managers would arrange for synopses or full scripts of new productions to be available on loan to deaf people in advance of the performance, and would advertise this facility together with an assurance that, to make lip-reading easier, seats for deaf people would be made available in the front row (preferably at concessionary prices). In conjunction with organisations for deaf people, theatre managers might also, with advantage, arrange for deaf people to attend a preview of the production at which, with the aid of an 'interpreter', important information on the background to the play and its production could be given, followed by an 'interpreted' version of the play (using sign language experts at the side of the stage to convey the dialogue to profoundly deaf members of the audience).

4.30 Much of the education and entertainment that can be derived from films is denied to deaf people unless the films have been sub-titled. In practice, therefore, many great films are inaccessible to them because they are not, nor should they be, satisfied with merely a superficial impression. In the United States an Act relating to the captioning of films, for the benefit of the deaf, was passed as long ago as 1958. It would be of great benefit if a film library of sub-titled films could be built up in this country, and the films made available for hiring by Deaf and Hard of Hearing Groups. We *recommend* that the British Film Institute should promote the building up of a comprehensive library of sub-titled films available for hiring, to which new British and American films would be added as they were released.

Broadcasting

4.31 Both the British Broadcasting Corporation (BBC) and the Independent Broadcasting Authority (IBA) are mindful of the needs of people with impaired hearing.

4.32 The BBC is making considerable advances in its sub-titling section, where three deaf people are employed. As a result, deaf viewers can now enjoy a number of light entertainment and drama programmes on television. 'See Hear', the television programme designed especially for deaf people, is now

Photo: British Broadcasting Corporation

Maggie Woolley and Martin Colville presenters of 'See Hear', a magazine programme for the deaf and hard of hearing on BBC 1.

entering its fourth session and has the great advantage of being very largely conceived and presented by deaf people themselves. On Radio 4, 'Does He Take Sugar?' is designed to cater for all disabled people, including those who are hard of hearing.

4.33 There is still a good deal of scope for development and in 1983 the BBC began a five-year development plan to extend the range of its CEEFAX sub-titling service. At the end of this period the BBC hopes to be able to offer sub-titles on all major pre-recorded programmes broadcast at peak hours. This would mean that sub-titles were supplied for some 35 hours a week, or some 4,000 programmes each year.

4.34 The programmes of the BBC's Community Programme Units under the title 'Open Space' are made by, with, or on behalf of members of the general public. Such programmes frequently cover problems encountered by disabled people. A television programme for mentally handicapped people, called 'Advocacy Alliance' is now being launched.

4.35 The IBA supervises and broadcasts the programmes created by 16 Independent Television Companies and Channel 4, and by nearly 50 radio companies, all financed from advertising.

4.36 Sub-titling of Independent Television programmes for the benefit of people with impaired hearing is provided by ORACLE, a teletext service on ITV and Channel 4. The service is being expanded. By autumn 1984 some 15 hours a week of sub-titles were being provided, available to some two million homes equipped with teletext.

4.37 On completion of a five-year research programme by a team at Southampton University, a *Handbook for Television Subtitlers*[7] has recently been published. This is a detailed guide covering style and presentation, special techniques, practical guidelines on editing of captions and questions of timing and synchronisation. The research team also developed the NEWFOR equipment which reduces the time and cost of sub-title preparation.

4.38 There are a variety of programmes specifically for and about disabled people. 'Link', made by Central Independent Television as a regular networked magazine series for disabled people, has been on the air for seven years and provides free transcripts of all programmes to those who ask. There is close liaison with the Disability Alliance and the Disabled Living Foundation. Networked programmes have been supplemented by a number of local programmes, among which Grampian's 'Sign Hear' recently won the Scottish Broadcasting Award.

4.39 Independent Local Radio (ILR) companies have great flexibility in catering for special needs and all applicants for contracts are asked at their interviews with the IBA about their plans for serving disabled people. A number of programmes, such as 'Contact' on CBC (Cardiff), are produced for and by disabled people.

4.40 'Action Line' activity is an important element in ILR services. Capital Radio's (London) 'Helpline', to take one example, broadcasts public service announcements for disabled people, and 'Helpline Special Days' provide on-air advice and off-air personal referral. Another example is provided by Radio Clyde's

(Glasgow) information packs for disabled people on access to galleries, museums, theatres and so on; they have triggered an overwhelming response.

Staff training

4.41 Staff who know what facilities are available and are able to offer assistance to disabled people in the correct way, can minimise most access problems at arts venues. In the absence of training, staff may very well feel nervous about their ability to cope with disabled people, including those who are mentally handicapped, and may in consequence adopt an unwelcoming, or even hostile, attitude. It has to be remembered that it is sometimes the least experienced member of the staff that the disabled person meets first - the junior at the library desk or the usherette in the cinema. The training given to staff should include guidance on how to help people with various forms of disablement to get the most out of the arts activity concerned, and also how to implement the management's plans for evacuation in an emergency. Reference to these matters will be made in the guidance notes *Arts for Everyone* but it would be helpful to managements if short training courses and other training material could also be made available.

4.42 We *recommend* that the owners of arts venues, including local authorities and cinema chains, should ensure that their managers (a) have clear instructions on the admission of disabled people, based on a presumption of access, and (b) give adequate training to all their staff on ways of helping disabled people including the action to be taken in the case of fire or other emergency.

4.43 We *recommend* also that national Access Committees should encourage arts organisations to initiate short training courses for managers and staff of arts venues on ways of meeting the needs of disabled people. *Arts for Everyone* (see Chapter 2.12) should find a place in the training material. The arrangements should be worked out in consultation, as appropriate, with the Arts Councils, Regional Arts Associations, Area Museum and Library Services and local authority Arts and Recreation Departments, as well as with organisations for disabled people.

Pricing policies

4.44 Among those regularly offered concessions on ticket prices at arts venues are children, students, old age pensioners and unemployed people. Many disabled people in receipt of allowances and pensions may not be able to register as unemployed, yet their financial situation is often comparable. Arts venues should therefore include disabled people in their ticket pricing concession schemes, as a number already do.

4.45 Some disabled people who may, for instance, be blind or wheelchair users, can attend arts events only if accompanied by someone else. Wherever the nature of the disability, the policy of the venue, or other related factors make this necessary, it would be helpful if, to complement concessions for disabled people themselves, managements were to offer either free or concessionary tickets to people accompanying disabled visitors. A number of theatres, including the National Theatre, have already made moves in this direction.

4.46 Wheelchair users often have only a limited choice of seat in the theatre, perhaps in the dress circle or in a box. Usually the seats are at the side of the auditorium and too often have poor sight lines. Other managements would do well to consider following the lead of those who offer seats to wheelchair users at concessionary prices if they have no choice but to sit in the most expensive parts of the theatre. The same should apply to people who are deaf or whose sight is poor with the result that they fare best in seats near the front of the auditorium, which are often priced the highest.

4.47 It may be argued on commercial grounds that it is unreasonable to expect price concessions for disabled people, or others, unless the places would not otherwise be taken up, or there are associated administrative savings (as with group bookings), or the cost of the concession can be met from some special subvention. To adhere rigidly to such principles would be to take much too narrow a view, but it would not be in the interests of disabled people that they should constitute a significant financial drain on arts managements, given the precarious financial situation of many arts enterprises.

4.48 Nevertheless, taking into account the low income-level of many disabled people, well-designed concessionary schemes can have a highly beneficial effect. We would urge strongly therefore that those who provide arts funding - whether from public funds or commercial sources - should include provision in their subventions for the cost of operating concessionary pricing schemes for disabled people, where the schemes cannot be so designed as to pay their way. Evidence from the USA suggests that season ticket concession schemes for disabled people, combined with effective marketing strategies, can sometimes have a beneficial effect on the box office.

4.49 In designing a system of price concessions there are a variety of factors to be taken into account. It will be necessary to decide, for example, what types of disability should qualify; to what extent different disabilities should be dealt with differently - taking into account that some disabled people may need to be accompanied or may even be required by the licensing authorities to be escorted; what evidence of disability should be required; and whether there should be more generous remission for those whose disability makes it necessary for them to go in the most expensive seats (or precludes them from sitting in certain areas, such as parts of the gallery). But the problems of devising sophisticated systems cannot provide a reason for making no move at all.

Managements may well find it best to start off with a rudimentary scheme which they will be prepared to elaborate in the light of experience and further consultation with representatives of disabled people.

4.50 Concessionary schemes may well vary from place to place, to take account of local circumstances, but there are some design features which could, with advantage, be incorporated in most or all of them. We *recommend* that national Access Committees should arrange for guidelines to be prepared by a working group with members from some of the main organisations of disabled people and from the associations of venue owners and managers.

Transport

4.51 Lack of adequate transport is a major obstacle to the involvement of disabled people in arts activities. For wheelchair users in particular, public transport is usually unsuitable. Schemes designed to assist disabled people take various forms and local voluntary organisations can perform an invaluable service by setting up subsidised or voluntary transport schemes. Nevertheless, many, if not most, of the present dial-a-ride and other voluntary transport schemes, however advantageous, have a common weakness when it comes to the arts. This is that disabled people have to book a vehicle for both the outward and the return journey, at least days, and sometimes weeks or even months, in advance. Informal and flexible arrangements for meeting friends - perhaps for a meal - before or after the arts event, are thus inhibited.

4.52 The operation of many transport schemes is confined within a district's boundaries and so arts events that take place in neighbouring districts remain inaccessible. Also there may be limitations on the number of journeys an individual can make.

4.53 Every scheme is different; some are costly, others relate their charges to those of the regional public transport service. Some will carry an escort free where a wheelchair user is unable to travel unaccompanied. Others charge full fare. Consultation with potential users as well as with existing schemes will be a great help to all local organisations considering setting up transport schemes for disabled people.

4.54 There seems small prospect, however, that voluntary organisations can do all that is required. There is therefore a continuing need for government and local authority involvement, as well as for transport subsidy schemes run by Regional Arts Associations. We *recommend* that the Secretary of State for Transport should consider means of fostering the best development of schemes for helping disabled people to get to and from arts venues.

Dissemination of information

4.55 Improved dissemination of information can be a most effective means of involving disabled people more fully in the arts. Already hindered by their handicapping condition, they usually have great difficulty in discovering whether the particular arts venue they wish to visit will in fact be accessible to them. The normal sources of information on the arts rarely give guidance on whether or not disabled people can get into and around arts buildings, or whether the management has any policies which affect such people - a policy, for example, that

wheelchair users must be accompanied or must book in advance, or that guide dogs are, or are not, admitted. It is a welcome relief to find a venue such as the Adam Smith Theatre in Kirkcaldy which, in its general publicity under 'How do I book?', advertises that 'the theatre is totally accessible to the disabled - in fact, we are proud to have two Special Design Awards. Guide dogs are most welcome. If you feel you might have any special problems, do please ring us beforehand'.

4.56 Sometimes, when information for disabled people is provided in general publicity, it consists *only* of a telephone number for the disabled person to ring, and experience shows that the person answering will not always have the particular piece of information needed. To take just one example, a recent spot check on a number of major museums showed that, when asked if their lecture rooms had facilities for people with hearing aids, none of those who should have had the information knew the answer.

4.57 To be completely effective, publicity about facilities for disabled people must be capable of reaching people without sight, without hearing, or without walking or reading ability. All possible channels of dissemination must therefore be used including, for example, the issue of leaflets, talking newspapers and cassettes through rganisations for disabled people, otices placed in doctors' and ospital waiting rooms, and local adio.

.58 Local access guides, roduced by a wide variety of cal bodies (including chambers f commerce, rotary clubs, scouts nd girl guides), too rarely rovide reliable information out arts buildings, and where ich buildings are included the formation about them may be mited to that relevant to heelchair users.

59 Those producing access uides need to remember that:

(a) information becomes outdated very quickly, so that arrangements for regular revision should be made from the start;

(b) guides should cover not only wheelchair users but also people who walk with difficulty, or whose sight or hearing is impaired;

(c) one person may not be able to look at things from a standpoint which covers the whole range of disabilities. It is therefore better that access surveys should be conducted by teams which include people with different disabilities;

d) actual dimensions should be given in the guide and not merely an opinion, as what seems 'quite good' to the writer may be quite impossible for individual disabled people;

(e) every effort should be made to publicise the guide and wherever possible it should be sent individually to those known to need it;

(f) disabled people using the guides, but who find it necessary to make supplementary enquiries, should be encouraged to state their requirements as precisely as possible.

4.60 We hope that the need for access guides to cover arts opportunities will steadily diminish as general arts advertising increasingly includes information of value to disabled people and is successful in reaching them; and as signs, such as that adopted for the Sympathetic Hearing Scheme, become seen more frequently on arts buildings.

4.61 We are glad to commend the work undertaken by the Access and Information Group (formerly the International Year of Disabled People Symbol and Listings Group) including their efforts to supplement the wheelchair symbol by additional public information symbols relating to various facilities for people with different types of handicap. As a pilot for other parts of the country, the Group has worked with the Society of West End Theatres (SWET) on, among other things, the inclusion of information on wheelchair and induction loop facilities in the SWET theatre guide, and on a simple and effective check list for box-office staff. In conjunction with Artsline - the telephone information service on the arts in London for people with disabilities - the Group has successfully encouraged 'City Limits', the events listings magazine, to include information on facilities for disabled people at the arts venues listed. *City Limits* is believed to be the first commercial magazine of its type to recognise the value of providing such information to its readers.

4.62 We share the view of the Access and Information Group that agencies funding arts projects should concern themselves with the policies of their clients in regard to the provision of information for disabled people. We return to this matter in the next chapter.

References

1 Department of Health and Social Security.
Access for Disabled People: English Committee, Press Release 83/205, DHSS October 1983

2 Rogerson, R W K C and Farquhar, A
Access for Disabled Guidebook, Scottish Council on Disability, Edinburgh, 198

3 Department of the Environment.
Building and Buildings Fourth Amendment (Draft), DOE, London, 1984

4 Department of the Environment.
Building (Amendment) Regulations NI 1984. HMSO, 1984

5 Scottish Development Department.
Building Standards (Scotland) Amendment Regulations, HMSO, 198

6 Association for Business Sponsorship of the Arts.
Business Sponsorship Incentive Scheme, ABSA, Bath, 1984

7 Southampton University Departmen of Electrical Engineering.
Handbook for Television Subtitlers, IBA Engineering Information Service, London, 1984

Chapter 5

General strategy for arts and disability organisations

5.1 Worthwhile developments in arts opportunities for disabled people can be secured only by the imagination and effort of a host of individuals and organisations, but well-designed administrative structures may help to stimulate and channel this work. One possibility might be to set up a wholly new national organisation, operating nationwide with a regional structure, to initiate and co-ordinate activity in this field. But in the course of our consultations it has been made abundantly clear to us that the creation of a new national organisation of this sort, with the pull on resources entailed, would be strongly resented by many members and officers of existing organisations. The general acceptance of its authority needed by the new organisation might well therefore prove to be lacking. Nor do we ourselves believe that there is a sufficient prospect that advantages would accrue to disabled people to justify the administrative costs involved - whether they were to be met from public or private sources. In our view, the better course lies in working with and through existing organisations.

The Arts Councils

5.2 We look first of all at the role of the Arts Council of Great Britain. The prime objects of the Arts Council, as laid down under its Royal Charter, are (a) to develop and improve the knowledge, understanding and practice of the arts; and (b) to increase the accessibility of the arts to the public throughout Great Britain. The Minister for the Arts has recently referred in Parliament to his encouragement to the Arts Council and all other arts organisations to take steps, within the resources available to them, to facilitate the participation of disabled people in the arts, including improvements in access to premises.

5.3 We believe that the Arts Council should now, as a matter of urgency, place much greater emphasis on helping disabled people towards a fuller enjoyment and understanding of the arts. We were initially surprised and dismayed to find that the strategy for a decade outlined in the Council's report entitled *The Glory of the Garden*[1] made no mention of disabled people. We were glad to learn, therefore, in October 1984, that the Council was considering the needs of people with disabilities, both as audiences and as artists and performers, in the next stage of its review. We understand that the Council is in process of developing a code of good practice on arts and disability for adoption by its clients and welcome this as a positive step.

5.4 We are told that once our report has been published, the Arts Council intends to have discussions with a view to framing a broad policy towards arts and disability. We *recommend* that, after consulting organisations for disabled people and arts organisations, the Arts Council should, within a year, publish a policy statement giving or reaffirming a clear commitment to the widening of arts opportunities for disabled people, whether as artists or otherwise, and setting out the means by which the Council will seek to achieve this, and the means by which it will expect its clients to do so. Corresponding action should be taken by the Arts Councils of Northern Ireland, Scotland and Wales.

5.5 We *recommend* that all the Arts Councils should make it a condition of funding that arts enterprises take adequate steps to serve the needs of disabled people in their employment policy, which we discuss in Chapter 10, in their educational programmes, in their access facilities, in the information they give about these facilities in their general publicity and in the way it is disseminated.

A good record in these respects should be known to count in an applicant's favour.

5.6 In each case where improvement is necessary the client should be required, within two years at the most, to prepar and agree with the Arts Council an action plan. Clearly, the period within which action on th plan was required to reach completion would vary accordin to the nature of the deficiencies and the extent of the resources available. National Access Committees are already concerned to strengthen the ability of local access committee to serve as sources of expert advice on access matters. These committees should be used by th Arts Councils and their clients t assist in the drawing up and monitoring of action plans.

5.7 All clients should be called upon to include information about access in their publicity material. Accurate access information should be incorporated in the listings-type material carried in the Arts Councils' own publications as well as in the publications of RAAs and of the clients of thes bodies. A system could be introduced, similar to that used by *City Limits* and the Society of West End Theatres' theatre guide, whereby access information is supplied by the appropriate organisation of disabled people in consultation with the arts venue.

.8 The policy statements to be issued by the Arts Councils should cover also their criteria for meeting funding requests from artists or arts companies wishing to work with disabled people and from disabled artists or groups. In developing these criteria it should be recognised that such enterprises may well be extending the frontiers of artistic experience as, for example, is the case with theatrical productions incorporating sign language as a means of communicating with deaf people. It will be necessary to ensure that those responsible for assessing the projects are sufficiently familiar with the relevant techniques and styles. This would be consistent with the practice now being adopted in regard to ethnic minority arts groups, where it is recognised that there should always be some experts on panels of assessors who either come from an ethnic minority background or who are knowledgeable about the area.

.9 Considerations relevant to the funding of arts projects involving disabled people are discussed more fully in the separate report we commissioned on this subject, as explained in Chapter 2.10.

Regional Arts Associations

.10 RAAs in England and Wales - there are none in Northern Ireland and Scotland - have been most helpful to us in our Inquiry and have already gone some way towards recognising the needs of disabled people. In 1983 the Council of Regional Arts Associations (CORAA) published a short pamphlet which included an account of the particular challenges the 12 English RAAs might be expected to meet in the course of the next 10 years.[2] Among the challenges specified was the need for RAAs to be involved in the continued creation of opportunities for access to the arts by disabled people. We welcome this recognition which is all the more important in view of the wide definition given of the scope of the RAAs' activities:- 'The RAAs'...policies and work embrace not only the crafts, film and video...but within subject areas include aspects which traditionally have received little assistance, eg jazz and folk music, popular dance, minority cultures, photography, murals, youth theatre, etc.'

5.11 Following the regional meetings which they helped us to arrange, a number of RAAs have already issued policy statements relating to participation by disabled people. We *recommend* that, within a year, all RAAs should issue such statements after consultation with other organisations, including organisations for disabled people. The statements, which should be revised periodically in the light of public response and comments, should set out:

(a) the means by which the RAA will seek to meet the needs of disabled people, and also

(b) the means by which the RAA will expect its clients to meet those needs.

The annual reports of RAAs should be used to record progress.

5.12 In this way, meeting the needs of disabled people would become a recognised priority for RAAs, as work with ethnic minority groups already is in some areas.

5.13 In developing their plans, RAAs should themselves have, and should encourage their clients to have, particular regard to the needs of disabled people in:

(a) planning, marketing and publicising arts events;

(b) taking work to new venues (such as day centres, special schools, hospitals and clinics);

(c) extending concessionary charges and clarifying their application;

(d) providing services and facilities for other arts organisations specifically involving disabled people;

(e) providing education facilities and workshops.

5.14 The need for suitable transport and parking facilities at arts venues, and the advantages

of concessionary fare schemes, should also be recognised. To make the maximum progress, RAAs would need to maintain close links with hospitals and health authorities, education authorities and, in particular, with special schools, social services departments and local organisations for disabled people.

5.15 As with the Arts Councils themselves, RAAs should make it a condition of funding that proper consideration is being given to meeting the needs of disabled people. If improvement is needed the RAA should require the client, within two years at the most, to prepare and agree with the RAA an action plan for remedying the deficiencies. All clients should be required to meet the needs of disabled people in their employment policy, as discussed in Chapter 10.

5.16 For building-based clients funding should be made to depend on the drawing up of an agreed action plan for providing, within an agreed period, satisfactory means of physical access for disabled people with arrangements for involving them in the arts activities for which the building is used. Similarly for non-building based clients, the RAA should concern itself, in considering funding applications with the access provision in the venues to be used and with the arrangements for involving disabled people in the activities. In each case, arrangements should be made for including information about access facilities in general publicity.

.17 The Arts Councils and RAAs would need to review their own arrangements to ensure that they were well adapted to making and monitoring progress in achievement of the new objectives. They might find it worthwhile to study the successful arrangements made by the Sports Council for promoting sports activities among disabled people. Carefully designed publicity formed an important part of these arrangements, as did the appointment of officers with specific responsibility for promoting the relevant activities and increasing both their scale and their quality.

.18 It will be essential that the duties of specialist officers concerned with the arts are defined in such a way as to avoid any implication of a bias towards segregated provision, though, as with sports, this can have an important place. The prime aim must be to spread consciousness of the needs of disabled people among all those concerned with the promotion of arts activities so that constructive attitudes are encouraged and, wherever practicable, integration is adopted as the goal.

Other bodies funding the arts

5.19 Policy statements relating to arts opportunities for disabled people should be drawn up and published by all other bodies with funds that can be used for arts purposes. Before settling the terms of the statements, appropriate organisations for disabled people should be consulted. We *recommend* that such statements should be made by government departments, by local authorities and by other bodies financed wholly or partly from public funds, such as the Museums and Galleries Commission, Area Museum Councils, the National Heritage Memorial Fund, the Historic Buildings and Monuments Commission for England (popularly known as 'English Heritage') and the Development Commission. In some of these cases the preparation of statements is already in train. Such statements should be made also by charitable trusts and commercial sponsors who constitute an important source of funds for arts activities but, in most cases, have not yet paid nearly enough attention to the area with which our report is concerned.

5.20 Although these other bodies which fund arts activities may not all have the same opportunities as the Arts Councils and RAAs to devise detailed action plans with their clients, we *recommend* that in defining their own policies in relation to the involvement of disabled people, and in settling the conditions on which they will provide funds for the arts, they should take account of the matters discussed in paragraphs 5.11 to 5.16.

Professional organisations

5.21 We *recommend* that, similarly, policy statements on arts opportunities for disabled people should be made by professional and other organisations whose members are concerned wholly or partly with arts activities. This would include, for example, the Cathedral and Churches Pilgrims Association, the National Association of Art Centres, the Association of Independent Museums and the National Music Council. We are glad to note that the Museums Association has already set up a working group to work out a policy and guidelines on ways of meeting the needs of those museum staff and visitors who are disabled. The resulting proposals are to be considered at the 1985 Annual General Meeting of the Association.

Crafts Council

5.22 We have not sought to draw a line between arts activities and crafts activities. Crafts, like other arts activities, are of at least as much interest and value to disabled people as to able-bodied people. We have been disappointed to find, however, that the Crafts Council is not equipped to provide special help or advice to disabled people on ways of adapting crafts techniques or equipment, as to

suitable courses, or as to the means of setting up in business for themselves. We *recommend* that the Crafts Council should make a policy statement committing itself to extend its activities to cover these functions, and that this extension should be taken into account in the allocation of funds to the Council. Corresponding action should be taken in Northern Ireland, Scotland and Wales where crafts matters come within the scope of the Development Agencies.

Arts clubs and societies

5.23 The United Kingdom has a wealth of organisations concerned with amateur involvement in music, drama, painting and many other art forms. Some of the clubs and societies make a special effort to encourage and facilitate the membership of disabled people, but most do not. We believe that the national councils of organisations concerned with amateur arts involvement should give a lead on this and we *recommend* that they should consider how best their member organisations could enable and encourage disabled people to join, and that the national councils should issue guidance to their constituents accordingly.

National disability organisations

5.24 Some disability organisations which operate on a

national scale have developed a network of local clubs with arts (including crafts) among their activities. We *recommend* that such organisations consider means of enabling selected club leaders and helpers to attend training courses in the arts, and means of making available to members of their clubs specialist advice on arts activities and training in such activities. In some cases it may be possible to get help, and the loan of equipment, from nearby professional or amateur arts bodies.

Integrated workshops by professional touring companies

5.25 Companies on tour are increasingly offering workshops in the localities where they perform. We welcome this and would like to see more people with disabilities invited. We *recommend* that co-ordinating agencies, such as RAAs and Shape services, should assist touring companies in making arrangements locally for arts workshops involving disabled people.

Periodical meetings between arts providers and disabled people or their representatives

5.26 From experience of our 16 consultative meetings, organised in conjunction with RAAs and Arts Councils, we are convinced

that regular meetings of this sort should become a recognised feature of the arts scene. We found that our meetings sparked off a number of useful initiatives and were effective in providing for an exchange of information about the various organisations and individuals concerned with arts provision and opportunities for disabled people in the region.

5.27 We *recommend* that, starting within a year, meetings on broadly similar lines should take place every two years, or more often; they should be arranged by RAAs in consultation with local authorities, library services and Area Museum Services, as well as with disability organisations and the Shape network. The chairman might sometimes come from one organisation and sometimes from another. Included among those invited to attend should be arts employers in the private sector, and representatives of trade unions with members in arts employment.

5.28 The meetings would provide a useful opportunity for sharing knowledge on ways of expanding arts opportunities for disabled people and would, in effect, constitute a 'standing conference' for the review of policy relating to the arts and disability. Representation should be maintained at a senior level, but people at the operational level should also be involved. The process of collecting information for, and briefing, the senior representatives of various organisations could be relied upon to have some effect in improving the co-ordination of views and plans within the authorities and organisations concerned. The convening of these regular meetings would also have the valuable side-effect of requiring the convenors to compile and keep up-to-date a list of relevant organisations. One of the subjects for discussion at the meetings would be how best to develop contacts between arts organisations on the one hand and disability organisations on the other.

Register of access facilities

5.29 Arrangements on these lines would themselves lead to a progressive widening of the arts opportunities for disabled people. But something more will be necessary to secure a sustained and determined effort to improve access to buildings used for arts purposes. We have already referred to the *Arts for Everyone* project we have initiated, in conjunction with the Centre on Environment for the Handicapped, to make clearer guidance available to those running arts buildings on ways in which they can help disabled people. This guidance will have a greater effect if arrangements can be set in train for systematically recording and monitoring the progress made in adapting arts buildings.

5.30 There is likely to be a need for some form of monitoring system for a long time to come, and a degree of experimentation may be desirable to find the best method or methods. The result to be achieved would be for registers to be compiled covering regions (or other convenient geographical areas) showing the access facilities available in each of the main arts venues. We do not envisage the establishment of a new national organisation to assume responsibility for such registers, but rather that they should be looked after by regional or local organisations (whether in the arts or disability field), and be available for use by RAAs and other funding bodies who would thereby be assisted to keep track of the action taken by their clients. In some urban areas it might prove desirable to appoint a full-time, salaried registrar, who could be financed from public or charitable funds, or partly from each source. But whatever arrangements were devised, the people made responsible would need to have the personality and the will to act as effective prodders and progress-chasers, and be ready to respond to (or channel to other agencies) requests for advice from arts venue managers.

5.31 In Scotland, and perhaps in other well-defined areas, it might be practicable to make an early start in collecting information about access facilities in arts venues, with a view to publishing full details in a single booklet.

Although some of this information is already held by the Scottish Council on Disability, and some by the Scottish Arts Council, neither they nor any other agency hold a comprehensive list. We suggest therefore that the SCD Committee on Access for Scotland takes the initiative to liaise with the Committee on Arts for Scotland on this matter. In consultation with other agencies, they could, with advantage, devise plans for co-ordinating the collection, collation, storage and dissemination of information on access to Scotland's arts venues.

5.32 More generally, we *recommend* that each national Access Committee should review the arrangements for recording and disseminating information about access to arts venues and should consider trying out in some areas, on a regional or other basis, a registration system on the lines discussed in paragraphs 5.29 and 5.30. If successful, the experiments might be extended so that the registration system would cover other public buildings besides arts venues.

Inclusion of disabled people or their representatives on management committees

5.33 One way of helping arts organisations to become more alive to the opportunities for involving disabled people would be to increase substantially the representation of disabled people on management committees. One of the suggestions made in our consultative meetings was that a place on each management body should automatically be reserved for a disabled person or a person representing a disability organisation.

5.34 We have considerable sympathy with this suggestion because the regular presence of someone appointed in this capacity - particularly if they themselves are manifestly disabled - can have a big effect in ensuring that management committee policies do not overlook disabled people and their needs. We have concluded, however, that a general rule of this sort would be unlikely to work satisfactorily. It is a tall order to expect one individual, whether disabled or not, to have sufficient knowledge of the needs of all categories of disabled people to be able to represent them satisfactorily right across the board. The needs of people who are profoundly deaf, for example, differ markedly even from those of people with a lesser degree of hearing impairment. Moreover, it is counter-productive to have anyone serving on a management committee unless they have, first and foremost, the ability to contribute to the work of the particular organisation and a real interest in the organisation's purposes and activities.

5.35 We believe that on this front, as on others, the best line of advance is to be found in forging better links between arts organisations and disability organisations, so that those responsible for nominating, or proposing the election of, members of management committees become accustomed to seeing that the committee's membership reflects the place of disabled people in society. When vacancies occur a special effort should be made to inform organisations with an interest in the arts and disabled people so that they can put forward candidates. But no-one should be appointed merely as a token gesture; they must be able to make a positive contribution.

5.36 We *recommend* that disability organisations and arts organisations should together draw up lists of those who should be informed of vacancies on management committees of arts bodies. The list of organisations used for convening the meetings referred to in paragraphs 5.27 and 5.28 could provide a point of reference. We trust that, in the result, disability organisations at both national and local level will be encouraged to pay more attention to the important role that arts opportunities can play in their members' lives. This will need to be done in consultation with the members themselves, so that their views can prevail. Where, despite the best efforts of those concerned, no person with a special interest in disabled people can be included in a particular management committee, there will be a special need to ensure that lines of communication with disability organisations are established and maintained.

Finance

5.37 Expanding the arts opportunities of disabled people will depend as much, or more, on the changing of public attitudes as on the provision of more money. Nevertheless, there will be a significant cost involved in achieving a number of the developments we are anxious to see - in particular, as we recognise in Chapter 4.17, more money will be needed for the adaptation of arts premises to make them more accessible. The cost of properly planned moves in this direction would be well justified whether the money were to come from public funds or from commercial or charitable sources. Such developments would reinforce the case for a substantial increase in the public funding of the arts, as recommended in 1982 by the House of Commons Education, Science and Arts Committee.[3] But whatever may be the future level of public funding, we consider that, within the arts budget, greater emphasis should be placed on the needs of disabled people. Our recommendations are designed to secure this - in particular, our recommendations to the Minister for the Arts, to the Arts Councils and to Regional Arts Associations. It is scarcely deniable that arts provision for disabled people has been sadly underfunded in the past in relative, as well as in absolute, terms; allocation of a higher proportion of arts funds to meeting the needs of disabled people could, therefore, be relied upon to improve the general deployment of the arts budget.

References

1 The Arts Council of Great Britain. *The Glory of the Garden*, ACGB, London, 1984

2 Council of Regional Arts Associations. *English Regional Arts Associations*, CORAA, London, 1983

3 House of Commons: Education, Science and Arts Committee. *Public and Private Funding of the Arts*, Paper 49-1, House of Commons, London, HMSO, 1982

Chapter 6

Local authority services and the National Health Service

6.1 The provision made for the arts in the social services of local authorities and in the National Health Service is uneven. The arts are frequently seen as an optional extra - in the social services as something to be added when resources allow, and in hospitals as a 'comfort' rather than as an integral part of the healing and caring process. Arrangements which are far more comprehensive and systematic are needed .

6.2 In some cases arts organisations have been able to exercise an influence from outside, but the complexity of administration in local authorities and in the National Health Service presents a problem for any arts organisation in determining the appropriate contact and how to gain agreement for particular projects. Arts companies, organisations such as Shape, and individual artists wishing to pursue arts activities often spend a disproportionate amount of time attempting to get leave to mount their projects or the allocation of resources to back them.

Local authority services

6.3 Local authorities seeking to assist in the provision of adequate arts opportunities for disabled people may be hampered, not only by financial stringency, but also by their own organisational complexity. In any local authority, several departments are likely to be concerned in one way or another with the problems of disability. Planning, Architects', Engineers' and Highways' Departments are affected by concerns about access; Education Departments by disablement issues relating to schools, colleges, youth and community services; and Social Services Departments by responsibility for their disabled clients who may live in residential homes, be attending day-care centres or be house-bound. Leisure and Recreation Departments where they exist may have responsibility for libraries and museums.

6.4 Our concern is primarily with those departments which can, and sometimes do, allocate resources and finance to arts provision, including, in particular, departments covering education, social services, youth services and community services. There is a growing awareness of the purpose and value of the arts in formal and social education.

This is evidenced by the growth and development of theatre and dance in education groups. The highly skilled work of the Young Vic linked to examination studies, and the help English National Opera and Scottish Opera give to schools productions, are examples of good practice. Both the performing and the visual arts can be of particular value to pupils with a disability, whether they are in ordinary or special schools, especially in assisting them to develop self-confidence, self-esteem and mobility. They can be of value also to the generality of students in fostering balanced attitudes towards disablement. The involvement of artists who are themselves disabled enables pupils and students to learn about disability and to appreciate the human worth and talent of the person concerned, whether as mime artist, writer, dramatist or musician.

6.5 Similar considerations apply with even greater force to social services provision. To take just three examples: the work of skilled tutors at the Dartington College of Arts[1] indicates the positive responses from children with cerebral palsy, or with other serious disabilities, in residential homes; the arts fortnight arranged by the Winged Fellowship Trust, using the services of the Highway Theatre Company in a holiday home, shows the unexpected talent revealed and interest aroused by involving the elderly and severely handicapped in drama and music; the approach of Theatre Workshop, Edinburgh in arts activities with mentally handicapped children, and with their parents and teachers, has demonstrated how a theatre group acting as a catalyst can produce something which is challenging yet relaxing, and also therapeutic. A further development is to provide training for residential staff keen to learn how to create a fuller life for those in their care. The support of senior management in the social services to enable care staff and social workers to learn about the benefits of arts activity is a significant and stimulating development, but it is still a rare occurrence.

6.6 The need for more systematic planning of arts provision will become even more acute as plans are implemented for replacing some of the present long-stay hospitals by community-based services. It will be important to ensure that hospital-based arts activities are not lost in the transition, but are carried over into local arts and community centres, with the attachment of artists and craftsmen as a regular feature. In some ways it is easier for people in the arts generally to reach disabled people when they are concentrated in a hospital or other establishment in the area. When they are dispersed throughout the community there is a special need to remind arts providers that disabled people may be house-bound or otherwise hidden, and in consequence more difficult to reach.

6.7 To enable mentally handicapped people to gain full advantage from local arts facilities, they will need help on an individual basis. One fruitful approach is indicated by MENCAP's one-to-one scheme under which a volunteer accompanies a mentally handicapped person to adult education classes and learns alongside him or her. But although volunteers can be invaluable, their efforts cannot absolve the local authority from responsibility for seeing that the move into the community does not result in mentally handicapped, or other, former patients being left isolated.

6.8 At present no one person is responsible within each local authority for seeing that the needs of disabled people are taken into account in the planning of arts activities, and there is no clear point of contact for agencies such as Regional Arts Associations, Councils for Voluntary Service, co-ordinating Councils of Disability and Shape/-Artlink services. Even where Leisure and Recreation Departments exist, they are seldom funded to an extent that would enable them to take on this role, and indeed they may not be responsible for the main development of the arts, other than for libraries and, in some cases, museums. Scotland and Northern Ireland, where local authorities are statutorily responsible for arts provision, provide an exception to this statement. It would, in some ways, be easier to ensure that proper provision was made for disabled people if this same statutory responsibility for arts provision applied to local authorities throughout the United Kingdom.

6.9 The need for further action to develop arts activities for disabled people was explicitly recognised in the recent report of the Association of Metropolitan Authorities on *Leisure Services for the Disadvantaged*.[2] We trust that the Association will play an important part in shaping developments.

6.10 We *recommend* that the Chief Executive of each local authority should take a definite responsibility for ensuring that the subject of disability is considered and discussed in the management group of executive officers in his or her area, and that there is a clear allocation of responsibility within the authority for arts provision with specific concern for disabled people. This function is not served by the present Access Officers, whose duties usually relate to the planning function.

National Health Service

6.11 We have been greatly impressed by the evidence presented to us, both in written and oral submissions and at the consultative meetings, that the arts in their many forms have a vital role to play in the lives of patients, whether they be in hospitals, health centres, day centres or in their own homes. The arts activities which should be provided for patients temporarily disabled by physical illness may differ from those best suited to the needs of the geriatric, psychiatric or mentally handicapped patient. As well as having great value as a recreational activity, the arts can have healing properties even when not used by qualified arts therapists for specific therapy. Qualified artists are now being employed by some health authorities and have a central role to play in developing this work. Arts therapists are, by definition, themselves artists and therefore the best allies of other artists wishing to work in the National Health Service or the social services.

Hospitals

6.12 Where artists have started to be employed as such in hospitals, the initiative has sometimes come from Shape or a similar organisation, sometimes from a Regional Arts Association, sometimes from a particularly imaginative hospital administrator or voluntary services co-ordinator, and sometimes from the individual arts therapist or artist or from a group of artists. The untapped potential for arts development remains vast.

6.13 The work of the Council for Music in Hospitals, the Tibble

Arts and Crafts with the 'Patients Activity department' at St David's Hospital, Carmarthen, where nursing assistants initiate activities for the elderly and mentally ill.

Trust, the Manchester Hospitals Arts Project and the many artists provided for hospitals and outpatient clinics by the Shape/-Artlink services testify to both the difficulties and the success of experiments. All too often, such projects are of a one-off or temporary nature and do not form part of a long-term plan for development within the medical setting. Where the costs of the artists or arts groups have been provided by an organisation such as Shape for an initial period, there may be serious difficulty in obtaining hospital funds for continuation of the activity. Moreover, although the results in particular cases have been very encouraging, the scale of operation over the country as a whole has been much too small.

6.14 Of all hospital patients, it is the so-called 'short-stay' patients who have the least opportunities to develop their artistic interests. Such patients may be in hospital for as long as nine months or more. In a number of short-stay hospitals, any arts and crafts activities may be provided by the occupational therapists with little additional resource from professional artists or arts therapists. Although to occupy the time and the minds of patients the library, the hospital radio service and the television have their own importance, they are not, by themselves, enough.

Art in three guises at the Manchester hospitals

6.15 Wider arts opportunities for hospital patients - whether short-stay or long-stay - can contribute to a more balanced outlook and sometimes may assist recovery. In providing such opportunities, the Manchester Hospitals Arts Project has made significant advances, already referred to in Chapter 3. Experience demonstrates the importance of having in each hospital a specific space for the arts. This should be provided whether the hospital is primarily for 'short-stay' or for 'long-stay' patients.

6.16 Hospitals for long-stay psychiatric patients or for mentally handicapped people, in particular, often have spare rooms, and certainly their patients have too many spare moments. There would be great advantage in each of these hospitals adopting an artist, or a group of artists, for a period of residency. The basis of the arrangement would be that the artists were provided with free studio or rehearsal space and, in return, agreed times at which their doors would be open to patients and staff. Regional Arts Associations and, with the necessary funding, any available Shape or Artlink service, should be able to help in setting up the arrangements and identifying artists who would be willing to play a part.

6.17 Such arrangements might extend to offering residencies to craftsmen, as well as to visual artists, theatre groups, musicians and dancers. The presence of artists and craftsmen in the hospital would provide inspiration for the hospital community and lead to the discovery of hidden talents among its members.

The need for new NHS arrangements

6.18 All in all, the present arrangements for using the arts in the National Health Service are far too haphazard to enable their full potential to be realised. For that to be achieved a strategy for the arts must be developed so that they are given a recognised place in managerial and budget structures, with proper lines of responsibility and of communication. In our next chapter we discuss arts therapy. Our concern in this chapter is with arts activities other than those conducted by qualified arts therapists in a clinical setting.

6.19 We *recommend* that, as an immediate step, the Secretary of State for Social Services should place a definite requirement on Regional and District Health Authorities to develop the use of the arts and to establish programmes for utilising the services of artists, especially those who are themselves disabled.

6.20 Incorporating arts activities in programmes should ensure that they are recognised when budgets are allocated. Augmentation may be available from other sources, such as

Regional Arts Associations, Local Education Authorities, charitable trusts, voluntary associations, and Leagues of Friends. But if these sources alone were relied upon, it would imply for arts activities the status of 'patients' comforts' whereas we firmly believe that they can be much more, and indeed can powerfully assist the healing process by the psychological benefits they bring.

6.21 The arts can also have significant practical advantages in terms of better use and preservation of buildings.[3] Experience has shown that people can much more readily find their way through hospital corridors decorated by artists, than through corridors with featureless walls. Certainly, walls decorated by murals tend to suffer less damage from passing trolleys, and can be less tempting for the writers of graffiti. It is an intriguing fact that the main staircase at St Bartholomew's Hospital, decorated with Hogarth's murals, has not had to be totally repainted since 1737. But more generally, the better atmosphere and improved morale which results from the discriminating employment of the arts in a hospital can have a profound effect on the attitudes of staff as well as patients and so lead to a more effective use of human and other resources.

6.22 We *recommend* also that each District Health Authority should arrange for a specially designated officer to act as a contact point and be responsible for developing relevant arts programmes within the authority, in consultation with Regional Arts Associations and other bodies such as local authority departments of arts and recreation. Such an officer would need to be of senior status. He or she should then be well placed to secure the backing of the management group, not least for the use of resources, as well as recognition by medical and ancillary staff, arts and occupational therapists and voluntary services officers in hospitals.

6.23 Each district should decide on its own method of working. But one priority aim of the designated officer should be to ensure that in each hospital an officer is nominated to take a special interest in the development of arts activities by, with and for patients, and to arrange for a consultative process for the sharing of knowledge and views. Sometimes there would be an existing member of staff who could take on this role, but in other cases new appointments would be needed.

General

6.24 Our recommendations in regard to local authorities and health authorities are designed to 'put the arts on the agenda' of these bodies. Despite some signs of increasing awareness of the particular significance the arts can have for disabled people, the general level of provision is disappointing - where it exists at all. We are convinced that it is a condition of improvement that clear managerial responsibility should be assigned and our recommendations in this chapter are directed to that end.

6.25 We *recommend* that the brief for any new hospital or redevelopment should include not only the provision of works of art and suitable display and exhibition areas, but also spaces for entertainment and the performing arts. A workroom separate from the ward 'dayroom' should be set aside for patients' practical arts activities. Individuals with appropriate experience should be co-opted to advise the planning team.

References

1 Ward, David.
Hearts and Hands and Voices, OUP, 1976 (See also *Music for Slow Learners* - report on the Standing Conference for Amateur Music/Carnegie Project, and a more recent Carnegie Study 'The Arts for the Handicapped', from Dartington College of Arts, Dartington, Devon.)

2 Association of Metropolitan Authorities.
Leisure Services for the Disadvantaged, AMA, London, 1985

3 Coles, Peter.
The Arts in a Health District, DHSS, London, 1985

Chapter 7

Arts therapies

Introduction

7.1 In view of the important part the therapeutic application of the arts can play in helping disabled people, we appointed three of our members with knowledge of this area to consider the role of the arts therapies as practised in Great Britain. They were Peter Senior (convener), Sue Jennings and Daphne Kennard.

7.2 The present chapter is based on the work of this sub-committee. They reviewed all the relevant written submissions made to our Committee, and sought evidence from groups and individuals likely to be able to help. In conducting their investigations the sub-committee took into account the wide range of arts therapy groups now constituted and also the variety of arts activities undertaken by non-arts therapists which are increasingly being provided in many situations for disabled people. Discussions were held with representatives from a broad selection of organisations including:

British Association of Art
    Therapists
Association for Dance Movement
    Therapy
Laban Centre for Dance and
    Movement

British Association for
    Dramatherapists
Association of Professional Music
    Therapists
British Society of Music Therapy
Nordoff Robbins Music Therapy
    Centre
and
College of Occupational
    Therapists

7.3 It was also considered important to consult a number of other organisations whose work might in some way relate to artists and arts therapists, including appropriate officers of the Department of Health and Social Security, the Department of Education and Science and the Chartered Society of Physiotherapists and Remedial Gymnasts.

Meaning of 'arts therapies'

7.4 During their investigations, the sub-committee were particularly concerned with the therapeutic use of the visual arts, drama, music, dance and movement. The use of the term 'arts therapies' covers the specialisms in these various art forms.

7.5 Many people have the idea that therapy is a form of 'alternative medicine', whereas it has always been a complementary aspect of medicine and healing, most appropriate for some people, inappropriate for others.

7.6 The arts have formed part of healing practice at least since Old

Testament times, as is illustrated by the healing rituals of non-western societies and the curative function of early theatre and music. Although the documentation remains scattered through manuscripts and receives scant attention in medical histories, the arts have been used in western medicine also ever since the Middle Ages.[1]

Aim of arts therapies

7.7 The aim of therapy is to bring about durable, positive change with someone whose development has been arrested or taken an abnormal path away from physical, psychological and social well-being. Arts therapies are a form of therapy in which the art activity and any resulting art form becomes a method for diagnosis and therapeutic intervention. These therapies are rooted in both the human sciences and the arts. The arts therapist is committed to the therapeutic use of the arts disciplines to further a person's emotional growth, psychological and social integration, self-esteem and sense of well-being.

Role of the arts therapist

7.8 The arts therapist can be broadly defined as a professional who uses an arts medium within a therapeutic framework as the basis for clinical and social treatment. Arts therapists have particular skills that can only be acquired through specialised training. The training is intensive and demanding, and the student will nearly always have completed an arts training course first, usually to degree level. There are a number of qualifying courses at post-graduate level.

Situations in which the arts therapist works

7.9 Arts therapists are usually employed within the context of the multi-professional treatment team and work in places such as day centres, special schools, prisons and hospitals. In many such places there are as yet no arts therapists, and certainly there are few establishments which employ staff covering all the various arts therapies; of these few, Fulbourne Hospital and St Lawrence's Hospital in Caterham have been brought to our notice.

7.10 Regrettably, employing an arts therapist is sometimes seen as a luxury, peripheral to other demands on funding. Nevertheless, the number of posts in the arts therapies continues to grow, which, given the present level of financial constraint, is a measure of the increasing recognition they are accorded.

7.11 Many arts therapists have to work in isolation (since in most institutions there is only one arts therapy post). Historically, arts therapists have had to struggle, and in some areas are still struggling, for recognition and the establishment of designated posts.

The relationship between arts therapies and general arts activities

7.12 We acknowledge that there could be concern if non-therapy based arts work were to displace arts therapy practice in hospitals, day centres, and other such establishments. We ourselves believe that both arts therapies and other general arts activities should take place in the same institution and that neither should be seen as a substitute for the other. Both require particular skills, specific to each, and should not be seen as interchangeable. We believe that arts therapies and general arts activities should be available within the health, special education and social services, with funding and resources recognising the part that both have to play.

7.13 We recognise that in some instances when the arts are being used informally with people who are disturbed, guidance will be needed from professional arts therapists who are suitably qualified.

7.14 Although we understand and accept the concern of arts therapists to establish a clear distinction between the nature of arts therapies and the involvement of disabled people in the arts in a more general way, we would like to see co-operation more actively developed between the arts therapy organisations and the rest of the arts world.

7.15 We wholeheartedly endorse the necessity and value of arts therapies in selected cases. We also acknowledge that there are many other disabled people who do not require specific arts therapy but for whom arts activities and experiences of many kinds are welcome, enjoyable and beneficial.

Conclusion

7.16 There are excellent examples of arts therapists working with disabled people in the United Kingdom. Our sub-committee concluded, in the light of investigations, that there is a need for a wider geographical spread of practice and for a more satisfactory relationship to be established in hospitals, day centres, educational establishments and other institutions between arts therapists and artists employed in a non-clinical capacity.

7.17 We would particularly welcome an increase in communication between the several arts therapy associations and other arts, medical, therapy and disability organisations. Our recommendations are designed to facilitate this.

Recommendations

7.18 We *recommend* that:

(1) To improve the co-ordination of policy at national level, the Secretary of State for Social Services should designate a senior officer in his Department to liaise with relevant professional and statutory bodies in promoting the policies outlined in this chapter; and that the Secretary of State for Education and Science should designate a qualified member of Her Majesty's Inspectorate for the same purposes in relation to education.

(2) The Secretary of State for Social Services and the Secretary of State for Education and Science should together initiate a comprehensive review of the arrangements for the practice of arts therapies, including training facilities, grants and job opportunities. The review might be undertaken by an educational institution with appropriate training, research and consultancy experience. To help finance the review, funds might be sought from a charitable foundation.

(3) The following should be among the objects of the review:

(i) to draw up a specification for a national consultative committee for the arts and arts therapies which would link mutual interests and promote standards. The Arts Councils should be closely involved in the work of such a committee.

(ii) To work out arrangements for health, education and social services authorities to appoint and fund jointly a qualified arts therapies officer at senior level to advise on skills, procedures and programmes. To provide back-up, the various associations of therapists should identify their own regional consultants to be available for liaison and advice.

(iii) To prepare plans for District Health Authorities, in conjunction with the social services departments, to set up multi-disciplinary teams comprising arts therapists and other suitable artists, covering a range of art forms. Each team could service a number of hospitals, clinics, special schools, day centres and community settings. In the result there would be a more uniform spread of special knowledge and experience than at present, and arts therapists could continue to contribute to diagnosis and clinical treatment where appropriate. Additional resources would be essential to ensure that the teams did not have to cover too wide an area. In each of the relevant establishments there should be a specific space designated for the arts, as we have already suggested in the case of hospitals (Chapter 6.15). This space could be used by artists, arts therapists, staff and patients alike, and serve as a focus for arts activity as well as a home for the multi-disciplinary team.

(iv) To devise a scheme, in consultation with the relevant training bodies, to ensure that courses in the medical and caring professions, and the relevant educational courses, have some input from the arts, including arts therapies. All arts training courses should consider arts therapies and the role they have to play. The scheme should take into account the need to make in-service training available so that a greater understanding of the role of arts therapists can be achieved at local level.

7.19 We *recommend* that the associations concerned with arts therapies should:-

(1) Consider means of disseminating more information about the work of arts therapists to those directly concerned, such as hospital administrators, nurses, medical and paramedical staff, teachers and artists, as well as to the general public. This would better inform people of the value and extent of the arts therapies and their availability, and should help the cause of the various therapy associations. An illustrated leaflet sponsored by the main associations would be very worthwhile.[2]

(2) Combine together to provide a forum for an exchange of views about practice, and to establish *joint* seminars, perhaps on a regional basis.

7.20 We *recommend* that all organisations for disabled people, and particularly organisations concerned with the provision and quality of care in institutions, should designate an officer with responsibility for the arts, including arts therapies.

References

1 Spencer, Michael, J.
The Healing Role of the Arts: a European Perspective, Rockefeller Foundation, New York, 1983
(Note also 'The Arts in Healing', a research study being undertaken by Dr Linda Moss at Manchester Polytechnic.)

2 Note the leaflet *The Creative Arts Therapies* issued jointly by the several arts therapy associations in the USA, available from American Art Therapy Association, Baltimore, Maryland.

Chapter 8

Library services

8.1 Libraries touch on virtually every area of human knowledge and experience. In particular, they provide one of the main avenues to involvement in the arts. Library buildings are often linked with related facilities and sometimes sited in a group of cultural facilities, such as a complex which includes library, theatre, arts centre and museum. Library services are increasingly being extended beyond the provision of books and other printed or manuscript material such as music scores, to include the provision of Viewdata (Prestel, Oracle) and the loan of pictures, audio and video cassettes and gramophone records as well as, for example, jigsaw puzzles, toys and computer software. This makes full availability to disabled people all the more important.

8.2 Arranging full access to library premises for disabled people presents much the same problems, and calls for much the same solutions, as in the case of museums and other arts venues. There are, however, a number of other matters to consider which relate specifically to libraries. We discuss these matters primarily in terms of public libraries, though they have application also to academic libraries and to private libraries run by companies, institutions or associations. There are two main needs. First, there is the need to make the subject-matter accessible to disabled people and to make sure that special materials and aids are available for those who require them. Second, there is the need to provide library services for people unable to get to a public library - usually a mobile library will meet this need, but sometimes it can be met only by the delivery of the library material to a person's own home.

8.3 In 1978 a report from the Library Advisory Council for England[1] examined library provision for the disadvantaged including among others hospital patients, the house-bound and handicapped people. The report drew attention to the good practice already followed by some library authorities but pointed out that disadvantaged sections of the community often failed to receive their fair share of the library's resources. Attitude and choice were identified as the key considerations in improving library services for disadvantaged groups and, among the many recommendations, it was suggested that all library authorities should review their 'outreach' provision to see whether more extensive services could be provided for house-bound and handicapped persons within present expenditure. After the initial publicity for the report, there has been little or no monitoring by the Department of Education and Science or the Office of Arts and Libraries of the response of library authorities or of service development arising from the report's recommendations.

8.4 In 1981, the International Year of Disabled People, there was a definite move towards making library buildings fully accessible, and while few library authorities could claim to have achieved this, many committed themselves to doing so.[2] A number of authorities improved their services to the house-bound, and at least one (Westminster) arranged for the production of a tape-slide training pack on this subject. In a few cases, magnifying reading aids were introduced for people with poor sight, or induction loops for people with poor hearing. Many authorities arranged meetings about their library services to which disabled people were specially invited.

8.5 Yet rather less than half the public library authorities consulted by the Library Association provided information about their response to the International Year of Disabled People, and undoubtedly an enormous amount remains to be done. To help authorities direct their efforts profitably the Centre for Library and Information Management (CLAIM) has now issued a checklist[3] on barriers to library use for the physically disadvantaged.

Literary aids

8.6 It was over a hundred years ago that Martha Arnold, herself blind, founded what has now become the National Library for the Blind at her home in South Hampstead. She started with 50 volumes. Over 350,000 are now available, mostly in Braille; although Braille was introduced in France in the first half of the nineteenth century, it was taken up only slowly in this country.

8.7 The Royal National Institute for the Blind (RNIB) is stepping up its Braille output by use of the Autobraille, a printing press capable of producing 1,000 copies an hour of a 48-page magazine. Music is still difficult to put into Braille, and all transcribing is done manually, but the RNIB is working on a process to computerise its Braille music production.

8.8 Talking books, recorded on cassettes, are a much more recent development than Braille. The largest talking book service for blind people, with 59,000 members, is that operated by the RNIB. The books are recorded on 12½ hour cassettes, so that a complete book can normally be held on one cassette. Talking books can be invaluable not only to people whose eyesight is impaired but also to people disabled in other ways which prevent them from reading printed books in the normal manner. The National Listening Library, with a United Kingdom membership of some 2,500, operates in this field and works alongside the British Library of Tape Recordings for Hospital Patients (BLOT). Special reproducers are provided free for the members, who pay an annual subscription for the loan of the special cassettes. One of the more recent entrants is Calibre (Cassette Library for the Blind and Handicapped) which runs a lending library of books recorded on ordinary standard tapes. The membership has now reached 5,000 and includes not only people with impaired sight but also people suffering from, for example, arthritis, multiple sclerosis or strokes.

8.9 Talking newspapers and magazines are published in a number of places, usually weekly and concentrating on local issues. In 1984, however, a new national service was announced by the Talking Newspaper Association for the United Kingdom. Under the new service, the National Newspaper and Magazine Tape Service for the Blind, the weekly digests of national daily newspapers are available, as well as Sunday papers and some weekly magazines.

8.10 In recent years people whose sight is less than perfect, including many elderly people, have benefited from the development of large-print material. This development owes much to the interest and support of libraries, and of the Library Association with its long-standing concern for the needs of visually handicapped people. Large-print books are now produced by many publishers and stocked by virtually all public libraries, but the range of titles is still far too limited to meet all needs. A small amount of large-print music is also available. A resource paper is issued by the Music Advisory Service of the Disabled Living Foundation; and the National Library for the Blind has facilities for producing large-print music, subject to the copyright laws. Recently the Associated Board of the Royal Schools of Music has offered an enlarging service for its own publications.

8.11 The Library Association publishes an excellent large-print booklet covering a wide variety of useful publications and aids for people whose sight is impaired. While economic considerations have precluded the issue of large-print editions of the whole range of books available in normal size print, the book trade is becoming ever more aware of the big market for large-print material. Well-directed publicity remains the key to realising the full potential of this market.

8.12 There are a number of technical aids for readers, including magnifiers, page-turners and bookstands. Information about them is available from the Disabled Living Foundation. Some libraries are trying out Closed Circuit Television Magnifiers, which incidentally have been found useful by students wishing to decipher obscure texts. Manchester Libraries have introduced the Kurzweil Reading Machine which converts ordinary or typewritten material into synthetic speech.[4]

Meeting the needs of mentally handicapped people

8.13 The needs for library services for mentally handicapped people have, as yet, barely been recognised, let alone met. The subject is considered in a report by Della Pearlman, published in 1982 by the Library Association,[5] which includes a selection of bibliographies.

8.14 A start has been made with the publication of books specifically for mentally handicapped people. Using a limited vocabulary, a simple structure and plentiful illustrations these books have something in common with children's literature, but those for adults normally avoid childish subjects. The audio-visual and audio material, including musical material, in some libraries can be particularly valuable in this context but the attitudes of library staff are usually the most important thing of all. Those prepared to take trouble, and explain things clearly and patiently, will find themselves

amply rewarded by the satisfaction and enjoyment that result.

8.15 Despite the modern emphasis on community care for mentally handicapped people, many remain in long-stay institutions. They have a need for library services specially stocked with appropriate books and other materials including audio-visual material, but adequate provision has rarely been made for librarians or library stock. Yet in some hospitals the library is the only place where patients and staff can meet on an informal basis.[6]

Use of library premises for community purposes

8.16 It is common for library premises to be used for community purposes and this can be of particular value to physically or mentally handicapped people if their special needs are taken into account (which will involve, for example, providing induction loops for those with impaired hearing). In the field of the arts, such activities may include group discussions, music appreciation groups, holiday activities for children, talks, lectures, exhibitions, concerts and theatrical performances. Exhibitions in which the work of disabled people is displayed can be of real interest to the community at large, and also help to build up the self-confidence and self-respect of disabled people themselves.

8.17 In response to the demand for advice services, libraries have been adding to their stocks of information material produced by community groups.

Hospitals and other residential institutions

8.18 In some hospitals and other residential institutions there are no libraries at all, and in many others there is only the most rudimentary provision. Although library authorities are doing some good work in this field, and their efforts are augmented and paralleled by volunteer effort provided in many instances by Friends of Hospitals or the Women's Royal Voluntary Service, there remains great scope for development.

8.19 The Library Association has been particularly concerned with information needs in the National Health Service. In 1978 it published *Guidelines for Library Provision in the Health Service: a consultative document* and in 1980, *Library Support for Health Care Services: a policy statement.*[7]

Proposed National Library and Information Centre on books, reading and the handicapped child

8.20 The Enid Blyton Trust for Children has established that there is a need for a source of specialist help on books for handicapped children. Centres in the United States of America, Australia and the Netherlands already serve this function but there is nothing similar in the United Kingdom.

8.21 We have been glad to learn that the Enid Blyton Trust is now opening such a Centre in London, in co-operation with Margaret R Marshall, specialist in books and the handicapped child. The general aim is to bridge the gap between the child with a disability which affects reading and those who create, supply and promote children's books. The Centre's library will be for reference only, but the aim will be to provide a friendly, informal and knowledgeable atmosphere for anyone wishing to browse or to seek specific information. Books on cassette, film and video will be included and various technical aids will be available.

Conclusion

8.22 Many library authorities have made a real effort to increase the use of their services by disabled people. There has, however been no effective co-ordination. In the result, initiatives have sometimes been taken in ignorance of relevant experience elsewhere, and there has been some wasteful duplication between authorities in such matters as the preparation of leaflets, booklists and other guidance material. There are, we understand, no data bases along the lines of those provided by the National Library of Canada, which list materials designed for use by handicapped readers, such as works in large-print, talking or braille books.

8.23 We *recommend* that the Minister for the Arts should seek the setting up of a small unit - perhaps by the British Library or the regional library bureaux - to collect and co-ordinate relevant information from all sources, including the commercial and voluntary sectors, and both to issue advice and respond to requests for advice on library services for disabled people; and that he should consider with the Ministers with library responsibilities in Scotland, Wales and Northern Ireland, how best the arrangements could be adapted for their purposes. We *recommend* that the Minister should invite the Library and Information Services Council to consider developments in the library services relating to disabled people and to advise on desirable action; and that he should include in his annual report to Parliament about the library service an account of important developments relating to disabled people.

8.24 The Public Libraries and Museums Act 1964, requires library authorities in England and Wales to provide 'a comprehensive and efficient service to all those desiring to make use thereof'. The Chronically Sick and Disabled Persons Act 1970, encourages authorities to 'make arrangements...for the provision of, or assistance in obtaining...library facilities' for any disabled person in the area. In furtherance of these provisions, we *recommend* that all library authorities should now examine ways of improving their library services for disabled people, including those who are house-bound or who are living in hospitals or other institutions, and especially those who are mentally handicapped. Library authorities should ensure that there is adequate liaison with arts organisations and with organisations for disabled people.

8.25 The Library Association, within its resources, has been active in seeking to improve library services for disabled people. To supplement its policy statement on Library Support for Health Care Services, we *recommend* that the Association should prepare policy statements on library provision for disabled people living in the community and on employment opportunities in the library service for disabled people (including qualified librarians who become disabled when already embarked on a library career). We *recommend* that the Association should take all practicable steps to ensure that in library schools, and in library training sessions, proper account is taken of the needs of disabled people including those who are mentally handicapped, and that enlightened attitudes towards them are encouraged.

8.26 We *recommend* that public librarians should maintain contact with local disability groups to gain first-hand knowledge of the needs of local disabled people, and should invite members of the groups to staff training sessions where they could explain some of the implications of disability.

References

1 Department of Education and Science. *The Libraries' Choice - Library Information Series No. 10* DES, London

2 Lewis, M Joy. *YDP, or Initiatives You Did Produce: Imagination and ingenuity overcome the obstacles. Library Association Record,* 84(3) p105-107, March 1982

3 Centre for Library and Information Management. *Checklist 6:- Barriers to Library Use for the Physically Disadvantaged.* Department of Library and Information Studies, Loughborough University, Loughborough, Leicestershire, 1982

4 Owen, David and Henry, Michael. 'Technology opens a new world for the blind', *Library Association Record,* 85(12) pp 458-459, December 1983

5 Pearlman, Della. *No choice: library services for the mentally handicapped,* Library Association, 1982

6 King's Fund. 'A library service for the mentally handicapped'. *Mental Handicap Paper No 3,* King's Fund Centre, London

7 Library Association. *Guidelines for Library Provision in the Health Service, and Library Support for Health Care Services,* Library Association, London, 1978

Chapter 9

Arts education and training

Introduction

9.1 Throughout this report we have argued that the most fundamental problems to be faced in improving provision in the arts for disabled people are not those of access and resources but of attitudes. These include not only attitudes to disabled people among the able-bodied, but of disabled people to themselves - in what they expect and in what they hope to achieve. Changing attitudes and raising expectations is a question of education: developing the skills to fulfil expectations is a matter of training.

9.2 In this chapter we look at issues relating to arts provision for pupils with special needs in ordinary schools, and for all pupils in special schools. We argue that achievement in the arts presents a fundamental challenge to common ideas about disability and handicap in schools. We go on to look at the implications for further, higher and adult education, and conclude with some observations on the professional training of those who work with and for disabled people.

Schools

Disability and special needs

9.3 The *Warnock Report*[1] points to the deeply ingrained idea in education that there are two types of children, the handicapped and the non-handicapped. Traditionally, the former have been thought to require special, and the latter ordinary, education. From the early days of state education, children with physical or mental disabilities have tended to be segregated into 'special' schools, on the grounds that they need a different style of education suited to their 'special needs'. Approximately 2 per cent of all children are allocated to special schools for this reason.

9.4 In recent years there has been a trend - greatly accelerated by the recommendations of the Warnock Committee and the Education Act of 1981 - towards educating children with disabilities in ordinary schools. This has been associated with a much broader view of special educational needs which includes many pupils who are neither disabled, in our sense of the term, nor in special schools. As Warnock puts it, special education embraces 'the notion of any form of additional help, wherever it is provided and whenever it is provided, from birth to maturity, to overcome educational difficulty'.[2] These difficulties may be physical, sensory, intellectual or emotional. Warnock estimates that in these terms, 'about one in six at any one time and up to one in five children at some time during their school career will require some form of special educational provision'.[3]

Disability and handicap

9.5 Special educational needs are not exclusive to children with disabilities. Moreover, special needs among disabled pupils may not be confined to their obvious disabilities. They may include social and emotional problems which result from attitudes to the disability. Nor is disability necessarily a handicap. Disability is the loss of one or more physical or mental function. Whether this is a handicap depends on the task in hand and the circumstances in which it takes place. Lower limb paralysis is not necessarily a handicap to someone working with desk-top computers. In this, as in many cases, specific disabilities may be irrelevant to the interests and ambitions of the individual in question.

9.6 Responding to special needs means assessing each pupil - able-bodied or disabled - as an individual, and not in terms of set categories of disability or handicap. Before discussing the essential role of the arts in addressing individual needs, it is important to consider a second, and sometimes related,

dichotomy in education, which concerns us just as much.

Two types of children

9.7 Educational abilities are still judged mainly in terms of academic achievement. As a result, all pupils - disabled or otherwise - tend to be categorised as one of two types: the academic or the non-academic. Although some pupils obviously do have greater academic abilities than others, there is a serious problem in this crude division.

9.8 Because academic achievement is the predominant criterion of educational success, it is sometimes assumed to indicate a pupil's overall level of educational ability. Those who do well academically are therefore thought of as the able pupils *overall*: those who don't, as the less able.

9.9 These two lines of division in schools - handicapped and non-handicapped, academic and non-academic - sometimes merge in the assumption that disabled pupils are *de facto* less capable of academic success and are therefore generally to be counted among the less able pupils: that disability means less ability in general. This assumption can become self-vindicating if children with disabilities fail to do well academically.

9.10 Disabilities can affect academic work, for a number of reasons. Pupils may have sensory or intellectual disabilities which hamper their perceptions in lessons, or motor disabilities which hamper their contributions. They may be inadequately taught. Their apparent failure may reflect teachers' and parents' expectations rather than the children's own potential. For any or all of these reasons, they may lack motivation, self-confidence and encouragement. Such children may have ordinary or extraordinary academic potential which is simply undiscovered. Their poor performance is not necessarily part of their disability but may be the result of attitudes to it. What is the significance of the arts in relation to these issues?

The variety of human ability

9.11 The *Warnock Report* presents a powerful challenge to ideas of special need based on rough categories of handicap and non-handicap. The Gulbenkian report *The Arts in Schools*[4] argues equally forcefully against the predominance of academic criteria of educational ability. We strongly support this argument, for we see an essential corollary: that arts education fundamentally revises the idea of disability and handicap.

9.12 *The Arts in Schools* argues that human ability and intelligence take a far richer variety of forms than is recognised in the conventional academic curriculum. Academic education focuses on particular forms of reasoning and the retention of information. Important as these are, individual children's strengths do not always lie in these realms of intelligence: and even academically gifted children have other abilities which can be entirely neglected in the preoccupation with academic achievement.

9.13 Some of these other aspects of human intelligence are demonstrated in the arts. Painters, for example, use visual media not only to express, but actually to formulate ideas and perceptions which cannot be comprehended so precisely in any other form. They not only express ideas visually; they are expressing essentially visual ideas. The same is true of artists in other media - sound, movement, language - each of which they use to articulate different forms of perception about themselves and the world they live in. Human intelligence and ability embrace all these forms of perception and understanding. It is the job of education to encourage them all and not to emphasise one to the exclusion of the rest.

9.14 This is not a criticism or devaluation of academic education. It is a recognition that the range of human abilities and achievements covers a very much wider spectrum than academic work alone, and that other fields of ability, including those of the

Bernadette Brown shows actress Elspeth Gray her prize-winning painting at the annual international art exhibition organised by MENCAP.

visual, performing and verbal arts, are as demanding, significant and valuable for children and young people. The current preoccupation with academic ability means that some of these broader abilities of all children are being neglected, while the strongest abilities of some may never be discovered. This argument applies to all schools, to all pupils. It can have extra significance for pupils with disabilities.

The importance of the arts

9.15 Talk of disability often emphasises what people cannot do. The arts are essential in education because they broaden our understanding of what people *can* do. Part of their value for all pupils is to reveal and develop positive abilities which are too often ignored. *The Arts in Schools* describes the importance of the arts in six principal areas of educational responsibility: in developing the full variety of children's intellectual ability; in developing the capacity for creative thought and action; in the education of feeling; in moral education; in understanding cultural change and differences;

A wonderful feeling.

and in developing physical and perceptual skills. These arguments, which apply to all children, are set out in detail in the report and need not be repeated here.[5] We do want to draw out some points which are of particular significance for the education of children with special needs linked to disabilities.

Individual needs

9.16 We have emphasised the need to look at pupils as individuals, rather than as types. The expressive arts are primarily concerned with clarifying and making sense of our responses to personal and collective experiences. A concern with individual qualities and perceptions is at the heart of arts education.

Expression and communication

9.17 The school curriculum is designed for the able-bodied. It relies heavily on speech and writing as the main media of teaching and learning. Pupils of ordinary intelligence with sensory or motor disabilities may have serious difficulties in these forms of expression and communication. Dance, drama, music and visual arts can release unrealised powers of communication in such children, and unrecognised creative and expressive abilities.

Raising confidence

9.18 The limited academic criteria of success which continue to apply in many schools mean, inevitably, that too many children, for the reasons we have discussed, can be instilled with a premature sense of failure. This can breed frustration, despair and, eventually, hostility to the whole process of education.[6] Rigid definitions of success and failure do not apply in the arts. Instead, they offer children and young people new opportunities for positive achievement on their own terms, which can generate a new sense of self-esteem, self-confidence and purpose in education.

Social education

9.19 A great dealof teaching discourages children from learning from each other. Work in the arts often emphasises group work and creativity. Dance, drama and music most obviously, but potentially all the arts in different ways, involve individuals working together on collective tasks. At best, this means sharing and adapting ideas and opening personal feelings and attitudes to group comment and criticism. The social, collective experience of the arts can be invaluable for all pupils, and especially valuable for those whose disabilities may have created barriers to contact and communication with those around them.

Education about disability

9.20 Our main concern so far has been with the value of practising and appreciating the arts for disabled pupils. The arts also have an important role in the education of all children about disability. This is particularly important in schools, where attitudes are often formed and reinforced. There is a tendency for people with specific, and often limited, disabilities to be looked on as disabled in general. This restrictive social climate can be the biggest handicap of all.

9.21 To have full effect, changes in policy and public funding must be accompanied by real changes in public attitudes. Such changes will become permanent only when children grow up with a ready acceptance and greater understanding of the variations and relationships of ability and disability. Theatre, dance, mime and puppetry have proved to be powerful media for involving and challenging all pupils of all abilities. Specialist companies, including 'theatre-in-education' teams in particular, have produced a number of tested programmes to promote discussion and positive attitudes to disabilities. We strongly commend the work of such companies as evocative and engaging methods of raising and developing these themes in all schools.

Special needs in ordinary schools

9.22 It would be wrong to imagine that all pupils in schools enjoy a varied and full curriculum in the arts which is somehow denied only to those with disabilities. *The Arts in Schools* was published precisely because the arts are denied too often to too many pupils. Our own recommendations are more likely to be met in schools where the value of the arts in the general education of all pupils is accepted. Providing the arts for pupils with special needs may need further action.

9.23 Even in schools where the general importance of the arts is recognised, many teachers feel ill-equipped to deal with the range of special needs they encounter. The task is to bring together expertise in arts teaching with knowledge of special needs. Since ordinary schools are designed and operated for the able-bodied, special needs can only be met by special effort. We suggest that this involves the formulation, by each school and by all departments, of a coherent policy on special needs. We *recommend* that as priorities such a policy should address questions of recognition; adaptation; and co-ordination.

Recognition

9.24 Some physical and mental disabilities are more obvious than others. There will be a proportion of children whose special needs will not have been recorded before entry to the ordinary school. It is essential that all teachers are able to help in the recognition of such children among the broad population of pupils, and to identify their abilities. Arts teachers should not only be involved in the identification of special needs, but should be equipped, through appropriate school-based in-service training, to recognise the central contribution of their disciplines to meeting them.

Adaptation

9.25 The aim of education is the same for all children: to develop their understanding of the world and their personal capabilities to the highest level possible. The broad aim is not different for children with special needs. The difference is that the methods and resources for teaching them may need to be modified to take account of individual difficulties. Warnock suggests that this is likely to involve one or more of the following:

(a) the provision of special means of access to the curriculum through special equipment, facilities or resources, modification of the physical environment or specialist teaching techniques;

(b) the provision of a special or modified curriculum;

(c) particular attention to the social structure and emotional climate in which education takes place.[7]

The child should not only adapt to the school, the school must adapt itself to the child. Integration is a process of mutual change and assimilation. We have described the central roles that the arts can play in making this provision. Fulfilling them calls for co-ordinated action across the boundaries of subject disciplines.

Co-ordination

9.26 Specific sensory or motor impairments in children may give an added value to work in one arts discipline rather than another. It may be desirable to give individual pupils extra time for one art form at the expense of others. This will require a level of liaison between departments and staff which is still unusual in schools. Discussion of such arrangements should form part of regular meetings between staff from the different arts disciplines, in the context of a general school policy on meeting special needs.

Ordinary needs in the special school

9.27 The situation in special schools is often the reverse of that in ordinary schools. Class teachers in special schools can have considerable knowledge and understanding of special educational needs: few of them have any special training or expertise in the arts. It is still the exception rather than the rule for a school to see this as a deficiency, since the value of the arts is not recognised or strongly promoted in either the training for, or in much of the literature of, special education. There are outstanding examples of energy and imagination. But even where the importance of the arts is understood, the small number of staff in most special schools makes it extremely difficult to have enough specialist appointments to cover adequately the various arts disciplines.

9.28 There are other difficulties, including alleged lack of local authority support. Special schools which are enthusiastic for the arts often complain of being left out of arts provision, such as visiting theatre companies, which is available to ordinary schools. Similarly, they complain of problems of access to resources including, for example, local authorities' stocks of musical instruments.

9.29 This unevenness in arts provision will continue until special schools, as we have recommended for ordinary schools, develop and declare a coherent policy to ensure ways of providing a full curriculum of arts opportunities for all the children in their care. To achieve this, as with ordinary schools facing similar difficulties, they will need support and advice. They will also need a steady supply of teachers from appropriate initial training courses.

Initial teacher training

9.30 The 1981 Education Act made no reference to teacher training. It merely placed a duty on governors and local education authorities,

'to ensure that the teachers in the school are aware of the importance of identifying, and providing for, those registered pupils who have special educational needs. (Section 2.5 (c))'.

A survey by the Royal Association for Disability and Rehabilitation (RADAR)[8] sought to establish what provision is currently made for this in initial teacher training. It concluded that despite many individual examples of good practice, 'at least half of the student teachers currently being trained have no specific training with regard to children with special educational needs'.

9.31 We recognise the many demands on teacher training. Nevertheless, we *recommend* that local education authorities should take urgent action to see that the deficiencies we have described are remedied through appropriate courses in initial and in-service teacher training. Specifically,

(a) Training courses for all arts teachers in ordinary schools should include compulsory elements on the identification of children with special educational needs.

(b) All arts teachers in initial training should have some training in the methods of adapting their techniques and uses of equipment for pupils with special needs.

This should involve direct contact with such pupils through visits and placements in special schools.

(c) The courses of all teachers in training for work in special schools should have a compulsory element on the aims and purposes of the arts in education. This should include experience of practical work in one or more of the arts.

Corresponding action should be taken by organisations responsible for the management of schools in the voluntary sector.

In-service training

9.32 Given the present deficiencies in initial training, and the pressing need to support the work of teachers in post, we *recommend* that all local education authorities (and organisations responsible for the management of schools in the voluntary sector) give a priority to providing for special needs in their programmes of in-service training for arts teachers in ordinary schools; and to the methods and purposes of arts education for teachers in special schools. Given the need to bring these complementary areas of expertise closer together we further *recommend* that, as far as possible, such training should be school-based and involve visits by experienced practitioners in the arts to work with class teachers in special schools and by special

school teachers to work with arts specialists. In the development and implementation of such programmes, the role of the advisory service will have particular significance. Here again there are difficulties for local authorities to tackle.

The advisory service

9.33 We recognise the pressures under which the advisory service works, and the increasing scarcity of resources which severely hinders its work in some local authorities. The levels of advisory support now vary considerably between authorities. Special schools are usually the responsibility of specialist advisers. Many of them have no particular knowledge of the arts just as their specialist arts colleagues may have no detailed understanding of, or contact with, special educational needs.

9.34 As a first step in promoting the liaison and co-ordination we recommend, both within and between schools, joint meetings should be held regularly between advisers in the various arts disciplines, with each other and with their colleagues responsible for special educational needs. The agenda for such discussions should include the items we have proposed above for school-based policy meetings, but should aim to co-ordinate provision between schools. In particular, we *recommend* that advisers should explore ways of exchanging expertise between arts departments and special schools through a system of school partnerships. This would aim to develop long-term contacts between staff in different schools acting on a consultancy basis to each other in tackling the problems of development we have identified.

Raising hopes

9.35 We have been arguing for far wider recognition of the unique contributions the arts can make in the education of pupils with special needs; not only in mitigating the effects of disability but in opening up new horizons of positive achievement and fulfilment to which the disability in question may be entirely irrelevant. Creating these opportunities in schools is essential, but it is not enough. When young people leave school the interests that have been awakened and the abilities they have found must continue to be provided for. Our arguments for the arts in schools apply with equal force to further, higher and adult education, as well as the informal education provided by the Youth and Community Services and Community Education Services. We are concerned that there should be a continuum of provision for the arts in education at all stages.

Further Education

9.36 Provision for special needs within further education varies a good deal throughout Great Britain. A detailed survey of the nature and extent of existing practice was published in 1982 by the Further Education Unit (FEU)[9] which we commend as essential information. We cannot enter here into a detailed examination of special needs and further education. We want only to point to some issues which have not been dealt with, nor often introduced, in the existing surveys.

9.37 The creation of an examining board dealing with both general and vocational education in the visual arts has begun to shape new patterns of provision. The Design, Art, Technology Education Council (DATEC), which is now a special section of the Business and Technician Education Council, has a range of courses for 16-year-olds and upwards. The opportunities extend to Higher Diplomas which are well regarded in industry and commerce. The place of the arts more generally in further education is very uncertain for 16- to 19-year-olds. In music, drama and dance there are many institutions, but few authorities provide a coherent link from schools to further education. A serious weakness in the current provision is the absence of sustained attention to the needs of those with disabilities. Few further education institutions have tackled the issue of providing the arts more generally for young adults. The exceptions highlight the uncertain attitudes of the very large majority of colleges.

The place of the arts

9.38 Given the increasingly distant prospects of paid employment for many young people, disabled and able-bodied, a recent survey for RADAR[10] reflects on the Warnock committee's proposition of 'significant living without paid employment'. The survey suggests that this may require colleges to move away from their established emphasis on vocational preparation to broader-based courses. Whether or not mitigating the effects of long-term unemployment is the appropriate motive, we welcome the diversification of courses in further education.

9.39 We urge colleges to examine the case for increased arts provision, not just as leisure pursuits, but for the more fundamental reasons we have given. In concert with this we add our recommendation to that of the Warnock committee that all colleges should recognise their responsibilities to provide classes and courses for students with special needs. To this end we *recommend* that:

(a) All prospectuses for further education courses in the arts should provide relevant information to applicants with disabilities and should, as appropriate, be sent to Special Careers Officers for the Handicapped and to the Manpower Services Commission for the use of the Disablement Resettlement Officers.

(b) Stronger links should be developed between students, careers advisers, disablement resettlement officers and disability organisations, such as the National Bureau for Handicapped Students, to collate information on opportunities in the arts in further education, and to advise intending students and teachers in post-school education accordingly.

Higher Education

9.40 Disabled people may be capable of the highest achievements in the arts. Opportunities, which in some cases are now denied, must therefore be opened to them in higher education, including universities, polytechnics and specialist colleges. It is not known how many disabled people manage to obtain places on arts courses in higher education in Great Britain. A limited survey of courses in Scotland was undertaken on our behalf (see Appendix 8) to examine the extent to which training in the professional arts is open to students with disabilities. The survey found very few disabled students. It is difficult to say whether similar results would have been obtained from a survey of music, drama, arts and other colleges in the rest of the United Kingdom which do the same job but are constituted and funded in a different way. Our general experience does suggest, however, that the disabled student is a rare exception.

Disabled students

9.41 Of some 3,500 full-time students at the seven Scottish colleges visited, four or five were severely disabled and another half dozen suffered from some deafness, diabetes or mild epilepsy. These students represent just over 0.3 per cent of the total. As a working assumption, we have taken the general number of disabled people in the population as a whole to be about one in ten. Carrying this proportion through to higher education, and even allowing that elderly people make up a substantial proportion of disabled people, the numbers of disabled students in these colleges still seem low. There are a number of reasons for this, including attitudes to applying; conditions of entry; staffing and support; access and accommodation.

Attitudes to applying

9.42 Disabled students are sometimes steered away from applying for arts subjects in colleges and universities by careers officers and by relatives, because of the precarious career opportunities in the arts. The tendency is to encourage would-be students towards computer and other technical studies. These negative attitudes can be compounded by those of over-protective parents if the course involves the student living away from home. Even strongly motivated students can be deterred from applying by the expectation that the college will not welcome an application nor be able to respond to special needs during the course.

Conditions of entry

9.43 The Scottish colleges visited said they treated applications from disabled students and from other students in the same way. In fact, there were two important provisos: that the disabled students could manage access to buildings and facilities; that they could do most of the course. The first does not apply to other students and is an additional obstacle for applicants with disabilities. The second is discretionary and may sometimes favour disabled students. Not all colleges ask for disabilities to be disclosed on application forms. Opinions differ on whether or not this should be obligatory. College authorities often feel they should know about disabilities before admitting a student: some applicants fear that disclosure will prejudice their chances of acceptance.

Staffing and support

9.44 As in schools, integrating disabled students into ordinary colleges is not simply a matter of leaving them to cope as best they can. Some measure of special support is needed, often in terms of designated staff. Most of the colleges visited did not make such provision, except to rely on the appropriate head of department or school to take responsibility.

Access

9.45 There is some evidence that access would be improved more quickly if there were more disabled students to cater for, but this is unlikely to happen until access is improved. Breaking out of this vicious circle will need expertise, extra money and the vision, will and effort of those in positions of influence. In the light of the Scottish survey and of other evidence available to us on disabled students in higher education, we see the need for sustained action in four areas: changing attitudes; policy making; better access facilities; and contacts.

Changing attitudes

9.46 We add our support to the *recommendation* of the National Bureau for Handicapped Students[11] that, as a general principle, employment prospects should neither be assumed nor taken into account by colleges in deciding whether or not to admit disabled people to courses in higher education. The only criterion should be their ability, with appropriate support, to complete the course to the necessary standards. It is for the applicants themselves to take stock of their own career prospects. Information on careers in the arts, and the possible irrelevance of disabilities to the prospects of success, should be more widely publicised and discussed within the Careers Service.

Policy making

9.47 Only one of the colleges visited in Scotland had a written policy on disabled people. Having such a policy helps to impress on all concerned that a college is trying to address these difficulties. We *recommend* therefore that all institutions of higher education in the arts should have a published policy on the admission and support of disabled students. Since attempting to impose a policy on staff and students might not change attitudes but harden them, we further *recommend* that all staff and students should be involved in discussing the need for, and elements of, such a policy. This process of discussion would begin the process of change. Since policy means little if it is not carried into practice, we *recommend* that, at least once a year, disability should be on the agenda of the governing body of each college for discussion and review.

Better access facilities

9.48 Once in higher education, disabled people should not be disadvantaged by lack of suitably adapted facilities. On offer and acceptance of a place, staff should discuss with disabled students any special difficulties and needs they may face in taking the course. Appropriate aids should be provided together with any necessary training in their use, before the course begins. We recognise that this will not be possible within the existing budgets of most institutions. We therefore *recommend* that a special fund should be set up for this purpose by the Secretary of State for Education and Science (and the corresponding Scottish and Northern Ireland Ministers) and that it should be available to meet applications from institutions on acceptance of disabled students.

Contacts

9.49 Colleges face many difficulties in meeting the demands on their resources. Their ability to respond to these recommendations will be facilitated by drawing on the specialist knowledge and expertise of existing national and regional bodies concerned with disabled people. In particular, closer liaison will be needed between arts colleges and the National Bureau for Handicapped Students:

(a) to exchange information on problems and solutions;

(b) to assist in the compilation and publication of a directory of opportunities for disabled arts students in higher education. Some of the ground is already covered in relation to music by *Choosing your music course* by Jennifer-Anne Lera.[12]

The examination system

9.50 The National Bureau for Handicapped Students (NBHS) has observed that opportunities in post-school education in all subjects depend on students being educated to an appropriate level to be accepted for the course. In most cases, this means passing a minimum number of formal examinations. In some circumstances, disabled students may be disadvantaged by their disability not intellectually but in the method of taking the examination. This can apply in the arts as in other disciplines. We *recommend* with the NBHS that internal arrangements for the examination or assessment of disabled students should be flexible enough to deal with the problems raised by disabilities, and that, where required, the use of amanuenses, appropriate equipment, or other aids should be properly evaluated and agreed well in advance of the assessment date.

Adult Education

Education and ageing

9.51 There is a tendency to think of the young outnumbering the old, and of education as primarily for the young. In fact, the number of those at school is falling, from 10 million at its peak in the 1970s to between six and seven million now. As Eric Midwinter[13] points out, if we add the many others who no longer have or have never had full-time work, and are over 55, we begin to describe the elderly section of the British population in terms of 11,12 or even 13 million (accounting for one out of every four or five people). This is of particular interest to this Inquiry since this section of the population also accounts for approximately two-thirds of all of those with disabilities.

9.52 This trend in the age of the population gives special importance to the provision of adult and continuing education. It is beyond the scope of this chapter to discuss these diverse fields in any detail. Fortunately, some of the ground has been covered in other reports which we commend for their detailed descriptions and for their practical recommendations. Eric Midwinter's study for the Centre for Policy on Ageing, *Age is Opportunity*,[14] documents the background and attitudes to, and the general educational implications of, these trends in ageing. He does not deal in detail with the arts, however, and we are grateful for the thorough analysis by Geoffrey Adkins (1981) emerging from his national survey of *The Arts and Adult Education*.[15]

9.53 Adult education is provided by local education authorities, university extra-mural departments, the Workers' Educational Associations, a variety of other national and local voluntary bodies, by the broadcasting organisations, and indirectly through the public library system. The local education authorities are the largest providers. This provision comes through specialist adult education institutes; colleges of further education; community schools and colleges, and off-site visiting teachers. Of an estimated 150,000 'non-vocational' courses in 1980, at least 20,000 were in arts or crafts, enrolling about 300,000 students. All the arts were represented with painting and drawing and, in the crafts, pottery and jewellery the most popular.

9.54 In recent years the implications of long-term unemployment, coupled to those of ageing, have accelerated interest in the need for education to be seen as a lifelong process. Within this, the traditional distinction between vocational and non-vocational courses has come to be challenged. This presents a favourable climate for the further development of arts courses which we are anxious to encourage. From the reports we have mentioned and the evidence available to us, however, we identify the following areas of concern.

Access and information

9.55 The interest in the arts among those taking adult education classes as a whole is considerable. However, the overall number, taken as a proportion of the adult population, is tiny. The reasons for this are partly economic. Of about 9 billion spent on education every year, only 5 per cent is spent on all part-time adult education. A National Opinion Poll has indicated that of the two million or so taking part, as many as a third are in the 16-24 age group. This is not only for economic reasons, but because many older people do not feel entitled to further educational opportunity nor do they think they can benefit from it.[16]

9.56 We endorse the broad conception of education as a lifelong, continuing process. We strongly urge increased provision of arts opportunities within this. In adult and continuing education in all the disciplines there is now a clear need for a concerted programme to publicise opportunities for older people and to press for higher levels of participation. We *recommend* that agencies involved with disability seek ways, on a regional basis, to collaborate with the providers of adult education and the arts funding bodies to mount such a programme and to monitor its effectiveness.

Content

9.57 Some arts courses in adult education have concentrated on appreciation of the arts rather than on encouraging personal creative work. A full and consistent programme of arts education will recognise both as complementary aspects of the same process. In the changing climate of adult education being brought about by the changing patterns of employment and unemployment, we urge those responsible for courses in adult education to recognise the importance of the arts not only as forms of leisure, but for their positive roles in providing new channels for intellectual exploration and the development of practical skills.

Liaison

9.58 Geoffrey Adkins has pointed to the diverse pattern of adult education, and to the corresponding need for greater co-ordination and liaison between providers of adult education and arts funders. The aims of this should include greater contact between professional artists and students in adult education. He has recommended that:

'Co-ordinators should be appointed at area and regional levels to advise adult educators and arts providers on available resources; stimulate area or regional meetings addressed to co-operative schemes and set up pilot joint venture projects. These appointments should be attached to individual local education authorities or to consortia of local education authorities. Secondment of existing staff is a possible mechanism.'

Such co-ordinators would need to see liaison with agencies for disabled people as a central part of their brief.

Other Professional Training

9.59 We have recommended additional elements in the courses of those training as teachers in schools. It follows that courses for those training for the medical and caring professions should also contain mandatory elements on the value of the arts in remedying the handicapping effects of different types of disability. As we argue in Chapter 7, information and training

should also be available on the nature and roles of arts therapies in the treatment in clinical settings of those who are ill.

9.60 We also *recommend* that the National Centres for the Training of Teachers for Further and Technical Education should include courses on the place of the arts in the education of students with special needs. An increasing number of lecturers are attending part-time City and Guilds courses, 'Teaching the Handicapped in Further Education', run at many colleges throughout the country. We ask that these courses should include due consideration to the issues raised in this chapter.

9.61 Finally, we *recommend* that the syllabuses of those in training as arts administrators should contain a briefing on, and some direct contact with, the handicapping effects of disabilities; on their responsibilities in addressing these problems; and on the strategies we have suggested for overcoming them.

Conclusion

9.62 Too often education is seen as a separate process from daily living, and the arts as a separate part of education. Our argument throughout this report is for those with disabilities to be brought into the mainstream of social life. In this chapter we have argued that a more thoroughgoing approach to arts education at all levels can help simultaneously to address these two sets of issues and to fulfil the broader purposes of this Inquiry.

References

1 Warnock, H.M.
Special Educational Needs: Report of the Committee of Inquiry into the Education of Handicapped Children and Young People, London, 1978

2 Warnock, H.M. Paragraph 1.10

3 Warnock, H.M. Paragraph 3.17

4 Gulbenkian Foundation.
The Arts in Schools: Principles, Practice and Provision, Calouste Gulbenkian Foundation, London, 1982

5 Gulbenkian Foundation.
*Introduction, Section 7

6 Hargreaves, D.H.
The Challenge for the Comprehensive School, Routledge and Kegan Paul, London, 1982

7 Gulbenkian Foundation.
Paragraph 3.19

8 Male, J.
Teacher Training with regard to Children with Special Educational Needs, Royal Association for Disability and Rehabilitation, London, 1983

9 Bradley J. and Hegarty, S.
Stretching the System: FE and Related Responses to Students with Special Needs, Further Education Unit, London, 1982

10 Bookis, J.
Beyond the School Gate, Royal Association for Disability and Rehabilitation, London, 1983

11 National Bureau for Handicapped Students.
An Educational Policy for Handicapped Students, NHBS, London, 1977

12 Lera, J.A.
Choosing your music course, Able Children (Pullen Publications) Ltd, 1984

13 Midwinter, Eric.
Ten Million People, Centre for Policy on Ageing, London, 1983

14 Midwinter, Eric.
Age is Opportunity: Education and Older People, Centre for Policy on Ageing, London 1982

15 Adkins, G.
*The Arts and Adult Education,*Advisory Council for Adult and Continuing Education, London, 1981

16 Adkins, G.
The Arts and Adult Education

Chapter 10

Employment opportunities in the arts

10.1 It would be entirely wrong to assume that disabled people can only be at the 'receiving end' of the arts. A moment's reflection will bring to mind numerous examples of artistic achievement of the highest order by severely disabled people. Milton, Pope, Beethoven, Delius, Renoir, Van Gogh, and many another disabled artist, are remembered for their masterpieces and not for the fact that they were severely disabled for some or all of their working lives. Perhaps because we are too close, it is not possible to identify figures of similar stature in our own time, but among contemporary performers the names of Itzhak Perlman, Ian Dury, Eric Sykes and Esmond Knight have become well known primarily for their talents rather than their handicaps.

10.2 In the many categories of arts employment there should be plenty of room for disabled people with the necessary skills and qualifications. Some will be employed for their artistic talents, and some for their administrative, technical, clerical or manual abilities.

10.3 Over the whole field of the arts, employers should commit themselves to providing 'equal opportunities' of employment for disabled people. This does not mean that a person's disablement would have to be ignored in deciding whether to offer him or her a job. That would, in some cases, run counter to common sense, as one of the main criteria of selection for any post is bound to be whether the applicant is physically and mentally capable of doing it. What the provision of 'equal opportunities' does mean is that applications from people who are disabled should not be rejected out of hand on the basis of preconceived notions, but should be examined carefully and sympathetically, and that disabled applicants should be given a genuine opportunity of explaining - or still better demonstrating - how they would be able to cope.

10.4 In many cases a particular applicant's impairment will not affect in any way his ability to do the job well. In other cases, where the impairment is of a sort relevant to the employment duties, the applicant may have ways of dealing with the situation of which the prospective employer will be quite unaware unless he is sufficiently concerned to find out. A person's motivation for a particular job can often be as important as the physical or mental ability to do it. In this regard, disabled people may well have the edge over other candidates.

Photos by Raymond Finney with East Midlands Shape

Playground mural painted by the visual arts team including seven disabled people, assisted by pupils of Shaftesbury School, Leicester.

Role of Manpower Services Commission

10.5 In opening up and developing opportunities of arts employment for disabled people, the Manpower Services Commission has a crucial role to play. The main functions of the Commission, which was set up under the Employment and Training Act 1973, are to provide a range of training opportunities and services, to offer an efficient and cost-effective employment service, and to provide temporary work for unemployed people.

10.6 The Commission has already contributed a good deal towards the employment and training of disabled people, and has committed itself to the objective of maintaining its levels of service for them. In 1983/84 special services to disabled people cost the Commission some £113 million.

10.7 In planning for the future the Commission has decided, among other things, to develop the activities of its new Disablement Advisory Service Teams in seeking to persuade employers to pursue progressive personnel policies and practices. The Teams will be able to draw upon the Code of Good Practice for Employment of Disabled People.[1]

10.8 Through its Disablement Advisory Service Teams, the Commission should, we believe, make a special effort to bring to the notice of arts employers the funds that are available for adapting premises and modifying or providing equipment for employees with a disability. Arts employers should also be made aware of the existence of Sheltered Industrial Groups and of the Commission's Job Introduction Scheme. We trust that the Manpower Services Commission will monitor the effectiveness of its guidance to arts employers on these matters, and enlist the aid of other agencies in disseminating information on them - including the Arts Councils, Regional Arts Associations, local authority Arts and Recreation Departments and Tourist Boards.

10.9 The Manpower Services Commission is responsible for two national programmes designed to assist people who are unemployed - the Community Programme to provide temporary employment and the Voluntary Projects Programme to provide opportunities for voluntary work. Our particular interest has been in the extent to which these programmes can help disabled people to secure arts employment or to become involved in the arts in other ways (through, for example, projects for improving access facilities at arts venues).

10.10 The Community Programme, administered by the Commission on behalf of the Department of Employment, aims to provide unemployed people with temporary work of benefit to the community. There are now about 120,000 places on the programme and a recent survey showed that 6 per cent of participants were disabled, 3½ per cent registered disabled. The participation of disabled people is encouraged by relaxation of the eligibility conditions, and we understand that high priority is generally given to projects designed to involve disabled

Photos by Raymond Finney with East Midlands Shape

Decorative panel in the Young Disabled Unit at Leicester General Hospital by the team including Paul who resides in the Unit.

people or provide support services for them.

10.11 A criterion for the approval of schemes under the Community Programme is that they should provide realistic work experience which will enhance the individual's employment prospects. In response to a recommendation by the House of Commons Select Committee on Education, Science and the Arts,[2] the Commission's Area Officers are now encouraged to consult the Arts Council or Regional Arts Associations when assessing proposals involving arts projects. But arts projects are only approved if regarded as providing a working environment, work experience and the disciplines of the workplace relevant to those found in outside employment.

10.12 We are told that no statistics are maintained centrally of the number of arts projects *per se* which are supported, but some 3 per cent come under the broader heading of cultural projects which includes heritage projects and work on museums and archaelogical sites.

10.13 The Voluntary Projects Programme aims to provide a range of constructive, work-related voluntary opportunities for unemployed people. Arts and crafts are regarded as coming into a category of leisure and recreational activities which are not generally sufficiently work-related to be suitable for funding. But exceptions can be made where provision is for the benefit of disabled people, for example where participants may gain useful experience in teaching disabled people and leading activities.

10.14 The Manpower Services Commission is responsible also for the Youth Training Scheme which in 1984 provided over 400,000 places, offering a year's foundation training for young people. We are advised that schemes concentrating solely or primarily on the arts are excluded, on the grounds that they provide too narrow a base of transferable skills, but that an element of arts work is acceptable as part of a larger programme. It is recognised that arts activities along with other activities can help to increase the confidence and social skills of disabled young people in particular.

10.15 We are sorry to find that, in administering their schemes, the Manpower Services Commission seems now to be taking a more restrictive attitude to arts employment than in earlier years. We accept that the Commission's essential concern is with employment and training for employment, and that to develop arts activities for reasons which are primarily cultural or social would be outside its scope. Nevertheless we believe that it would be consistent with the Commission's proper role to adopt a more forthcoming attitude to supporting arts projects which involve disabled people.

10.16 The range of employment possibilities for disabled people

tends to be narrower than that for other people and, partly no doubt for this reason, they remain unemployed, on average, for twice as long as their able-bodied counterparts. It follows that where disabled people wish to establish their ability and aptitude to follow arts employment, it is particularly important that they should be given the chance to do so. In practice, their opportunities for developing such abilities are fewer than those of able-bodied people.

10.17 This point is illustrated by the experience of the Graeae Theatre Company, a professional group of disabled actors and actresses. The company has found that it has to do its own training, in view of the lack of disabled people who have been able to get training at drama schools. This adds substantially to costs and makes it more difficult for the company to maintain its activities even at the present level. In cases such as this, experience of working in an arts project could have a direct effect in improving the disabled person's chance of gaining longer-term employment.

10.18 Projects involving the painting of murals by teams made up wholly or partly of disabled people provide another example of an arts activity which may have the direct effect of making a disabled person more employable; and to the extent that the disabled person's confidence is built up, his or her improved prospects may not be limited to directly analogous employment. Yet, since January 1984, the Manpower Services Commission has no longer been willing to provide support, under the Community Programme, for the painting of murals or the creation of new works of art by way of fresco or mosaic work - on the grounds that there is insufficient community benefit of practical value. We cannot understand the justification for this.

10.19 There are two more general points we wish to make about the Commission's schemes. The first is that the Commission should, in our view, do more to ensure that, so far as is practicable, potential schemes brought to them by sponsors will be accessible to disabled people, and that the publicity will make this clear. The second is to recognise that a good deal of work helpful to disabled people's involvement in the arts has already been carried out under the Commission's schemes. For example, under the Community Programme work in museums has included the creation of pathways and ramps to make easier access for disabled people, and under the Voluntary Projects Programme the current projects include an Arts and Crafts Centre for the Disabled (at Stockton, Cleveland) where unemployed volunteers are able to work with and train disabled people in a variety of crafts and skills, and (at Bridgend, Mid Glamorgan) a Gateway Club where unemployed volunteers can be trained to work with mentally handicapped people and teach them special activity skills in music, drama, dance, art or basic literacy.

10.20 We commend this type of activity which brings benefits to disabled people, and hope that the Commission will consolidate and expand these areas of its work.

Conclusions relating to the Manpower Services Commision

10.21 The Manpower Services Commission has made and supported some useful initiatives in regard to arts employment for disabled people, and in helping to improve access facilities. But we have found evidence of considerable unease among arts organisations about the restrictions and about prospects for future progress.

10.22 We *recommend* that the Secretary of State for Employment should establish with the Manpower Services Commission (a) the best means by which they can expand arts training and arts employment opportunities for disabled people; and (b) in consultation with national Access Committees, how the improvement of access facilities to arts venues under the Commission's programmes can best be developed in accordance with an overall plan. We *recommend* that the Manpower Services Commission should seek to ensure that potential schemes brought to it by sponsors will be accessible to disabled people, and that this will be made clear in each project's publicity.

Disabled people in arts employment

10.23 We hope that arts employers will be among the leaders in applying the Code of Good Practice for Employment of Disabled People, drawn up by the Manpower Services Commission. We *recommend* that all arts employers, and all professional associations with members in arts employment, should formally adhere to this Code.

10.24 We are glad to know that some arts employers are already trying to follow an 'equal opportunities' policy in relation to disabled people. The British Broadcasting Corporation is such an employer, and considers candidates for posts on the basis of their qualifications and experience in an open competitive system, though safety problems are sometimes held to preclude employment of some disabled people in particular areas. The Independent Broadcasting Authority also gives the fullest consideration to applications from disabled people, and policy on this matter is discussed with the independent television and radio companies through the Standing Consultative Committee for Television and the Radio Consultative Committee.

10.25 The largest employers in arts-related professions are local authorities with staff in, for example, museums, libraries and theatres, yet they have often failed to employ even the legal 'quota' of disabled people, when they should be giving the lead to others. We note that the Manpower Services Commission is looking at ways of making existing 'quota' legislation more effective.

10.26 Whether someone is retrained after the onset of disability often depends on the availability of suitable advice, and on how supportive is the attitude of people with skills in rehabilitation. We have heard it suggested that even some of the national disability organisations tend to narrow unnecessarily the employment expectations of their clients to unskilled or semi-skilled factory or clerical work. Better information is needed on arts-related training and employment for passing on to their clients by careers and employment advisers.

10.27 Organisations responsible for encouraging the development of employment opportunities in the arts and crafts, such as the Crafts Council and the Council for Small Industries in Rural Areas, have enormous scope for working with organisations of disabled people to provide advice on job opportunities and on the setting up of a business and on marketing. We have already referred, in Chapter 5.22, to the need for an extension of the Craft Council's activities to cover this area, and for corresponding action in Northern Ireland, Scotland and Wales.

10.28 We are glad to know that Equity has set up a Disabled Performers' Committee with the function of seeking out ways and means of helping their members who are disabled. By compiling a register of their disabled members, Equity hopes to avoid a situation where an able-bodied actor is recruited to play the role of a disabled person when there are disabled actors available of equal acting ability. We understand that the difficulty of getting adequate insurance cover for disabled actors has sometimes stood in the way of their employment. We *recommend* that, if further difficulties are experienced, representatives of employers and trade unions should take the initiative in discussing with insurance companies the best means of arriving at satisfactory arrangements.

10.29 A concerted and determined effort is needed by everyone involved in the performing arts to see that the maximum encouragement is given to the employment of disabled people as performers and in other capacities. This will require not only a more imaginative outlook in some of those who select performers but also the full co-operation of stage-hands and others who provide ancillary services. We *recommend* that (a) those trade unions with members in the performing arts should define and promulgate their policies on ways of maximising the employment of those of their own actual or potential members who are disabled; and (b) the Trades Union Congress should give a lead to its member unions on this.

Representation of disabled people in the media

10.30 The use of disabled people as performers is tied up with the more general question of the depiction of disabled people in the media. The influence of the mass media on the climate of opinion in today's world has led us to consider whether more constructive attitudes towards disabled people might be engendered if their presentation in the media were somehow different. We doubt whether it would be practicable or desirable to secure observance of a comprehensive 'code of conduct' on the portrayal of disabled people, but we should like to mention one general, and rather obvious, point which those responsible for the making of film, TV or radio programmes could usefully keep in mind.

10.31 A regular anxiety of most disabled people is that, in every way possible, they should be able to lead normal lives in society, and should not be treated or regarded as constituting a separate group of their own. Development of such an attitude may be assisted to the extent that people with evident disabilities are used in the media in roles and situations where their disablement is not the most important thing about them. One encouraging example of what we have in mind is the inclusion of Nina, a child with Down's Syndrome, in the TV 'Crossroads' series.

10.32 As another sign of a movement in this direction we welcome those TV programmes in which very little, or nothing, is made of the fact that a person being interviewed is confined to a wheelchair. Similarly, we should like to see disabled people more often taking part in TV panel games. Indeed, we believe that throughout the media - in advertising as well as in entertainment - disabled people should be used in prominent roles, and in supporting roles, without any implication that it is their disablement which has led to their selection. Disabled people are as much a part of the everyday world as members of ethnic minorities - whose greater use in the media is a welcome development.

10.33 Fuller integration of disabled people in programmes would also make it more natural for their needs to be taken into account when critics are discussing exhibitions, performances and other arts activities. If adequate provision is not made for disabled people to participate in specific activities that should be a matter for comment by the critics.

10.34 We *recommend* that the British Broadcasting Corporation and the Independent Broadcasting Authority should publish policy statements on the involvement of disabled people in all types of programmes, including audience participation and all aspects of programme production.

10.35 The growth of new technologies in the media has opened up opportunities for smaller groups of people to put their own programmes together, and local radio and television often have facilities to help them do this. We hope that groups of (or including) disabled people will make full use of these facilities.

References

1 Manpower Services Commission. *Code of Good Practice on the Employment of Disabled People*, MSC, Sheffield, 1984 (Obtainable from Disablement Advisory Services Manager at local Job Centre)

2 House of Commons: Education, Science and Arts Committee. *Public and Private Funding of the Arts*, Paper 49-1, House of Commons, London, HMSO, 1982

Chapter 11

Northern Ireland, Scotland and Wales

Northern Ireland

Leisure and Recreation

11.1 At local government level, two bodies in Northern Ireland have a statutory responsibility to provide for the arts. These are, first, district councils and, second, education and library boards. Their dual responsibilities extend to the provision of 'recreation, social, physical and cultural activities' and are laid down in the 1973 Recreation and Youth Services Order[1] and the 1972 Education and Library Order.[2]

11.2 District councils have responsibility for halls and other public buildings which house arts events from time to time, and while it is clear that the financial resources of councils vary greatly, many districts have sought to discharge their statutory duty to provide recreation facilities through the provision of leisure centres. All leisure centres are built to be accessible and, besides providing a variety of facilities for sporting activities, they are intended for use by local groups and clubs as a centre or base and to have flexible space for casual use.

11.3 The extent to which arts events and activities are found in leisure centres depends on a combination of local demand and management commitment. Their success depends on effective promotion not only with regular centre users but also with a wider public. However, being accessible, as few purely arts buildings are, leisure centres are capable of providing disabled people with new opportunities to be involved in the arts - by housing local arts clubs and societies or wheelchair dancing groups, receiving touring exhibitions and performances, sponsoring arts residencies and so on. In order to encourage the growth of arts activities in leisure centres and the full participation of people with disabilities, we *recommend* that the Association of Local Authorities of Northern Ireland should initiate discussions with arts promoters, disabled people and leisure centre managers. Examples of good practice could usefully be made available to interested groups to further encourage development.[3]

11.4 Because two separate authorities have responsibilities for leisure and recreation, overlaps in provision are likely and there are opportunities for shared funding initiatives. These could be particularly valuable for district councils with small budgets who, through providing accessible, flexible space in leisure centres, could co-operate with education and library boards and the Arts Council of Northern Ireland to encourage new initiatives for involving disabled people in the arts.

Arts Council of Northern Ireland

11.5 The Arts Council of Northern Ireland (ACNI) pays particular attention in assessing plans for new arts buildings as to whether provision for people with disabilities is planned. A new building regulation[4] requires provision of access facilities in new buildings, so far as the ground floor is concerned. In addition, through discussions with the Department of Health and Social Services (DHSS), the Arts Council is involved in a new initiative to establish an arts service based in the new City Hospital in Belfast. The Council has in the past provided funds for musicians to perform, through Live Music Now and the Council for Music in Hospitals, in various health and education establishments.

11.6 The Arts Council also funds and manages two schemes with particular potential to involve young people with disabilities in the arts - the Youth Drama Scheme and the Community Drama Scheme. There are obvious difficulties regarding access but we do not believe that these should stand in the way of encouraging the full involvement of disabled people in local and community initiatives in the arts. In particular, PHAB clubs are actively interested in extending their involvement in the arts and in Londonderry a group of deaf people have recently been involved in moves to set up a theatre of the deaf. The involvement of members of such groups in schemes run by the Arts Council should be sought.

11.7 In order to extend its own ability to make sound judgements about applications from groups wishing to work with disabled people, or from disabled artists, the ACNI is prepared to nominate a senior member of staff onto a proposed independent group which would seek to encourage and co-ordinate developments involving disabled people in the arts. We commend this initiative and urge that an attempt should also be made to find suitable disabled people to fill positions on advisory committees.

Arts therapies

11.8 At present there are no more than three or four art therapists employed in health and social services settings in

Northern Ireland, and no fully qualified music therapist is employed except the holder of the temporary appointment referred to in paragraph 11.11 below.

Art therapy

11.9 The Northern Ireland Group for Art as Therapy, established in 1975, has provided a continuing programme of short courses for professionals in related areas of work as well as input to various psychiatric, geriatric and other institutions, mostly on a part-time basis. The work of this group is made more difficult by problems of professional isolation and insecurity because of the small number of practising art therapists and limited job opportunities within the statutory services. Furthermore, because no full-time professional training course in art therapy exists in Northern Ireland, there are real difficulties in expanding the number of qualified therapists and therapy appointments in the Health and Social Services Boards. Post-graduate training must at present be sought in England and secondment or grant-funding be found.

11.10 There is a case for developing art therapy training in Northern Ireland in response to existing practitioners' needs and allied to existing arts chool training and occupational therapy training. However, because of the need to ensure that therapists attain and adhere to commonly agreed standards and principles it is important to acquire validation for any training offered. Only then will art therapy be able to develop with confidence and attract the necessary interest and commitment from medical staff.

Music therapy

11.11 The growth of interest in music therapy owes much to the work of a voluntary group, the Ad Hoc Committee on Music and the Handicapped, which was set up in 1982 through the interest of a consultant neurologist. The Committee has initiated a number of innovative projects to develop the use of music in the education, training and care of people with disabilities, one of which was to secure funds from the Eastern and Northern Health Boards and a number of voluntary sources to employ a professional music therapist. The appointment was initially for six months, but that period has been extended for a further six months with funds from charitable sources.

11.12 Hospitals which have had the services of the music therapist are enthusiastic about the work but, in the absence of any source of permanent funding, no plans exist to extend or develop the use of music therapy in health and social services settings. In March 1985, when the pilot scheme has ended, a report on the work and its effects will be submitted to the Department of Health and Social Services (DHSS) and we hope that serious consideration will be given by the Department to encouraging further developments in music therapy in Northern Ireland.

Additional developments in music

11.13 The Ad Hoc Committee gathered information about the use of music in work with handicapped people in Northern Ireland through a widely distributed questionnaire. Replies revealed a significant need for help and advice, training and equipment among a wide range of professionals. This stimulated the Committee to initiate a one-year appointment under the government Action for Community Employment (ACE) scheme in order to develop strategies for satisfying the needs that had been revealed and to offer suggestions as to how existing organisations could cater for this area of interest. The ACE scheme is now complete and a report on its work and findings is soon to be published. We hope that the various training and service agencies will take on board the findings of this report and look at ways of co-ordinating suggested development. Initiatives for 1985 include a two-day workshop planned with the assistance of the Tibble Trust and a residential music exchange as part of European Music Year.

11.14 The Ad Hoc Committee now believes that, as a voluntary group, it has done as much as it can and that its present work can best be consolidated by a constituted body with adequate resources of staff and funding to co-ordinate and extend the now considerable bulk of administration and fundraising involved in its projects.

11.15 The initiatives described have been in music, brought about by a group with a strong commitment to that art form, but other art forms could bring comparable rewards given an equivalent concentration of effort and determination.

General development in the arts

11.16 The need for development is urgent, with the various existing initiatives due to end in the summer of 1985. Accordingly, we *recommend* that interested organisations and individuals be brought together by the Northern Ireland Council for the Handicapped (NICH) to discuss the most appropriate form for a new development and to draw up a development plan for a three-year pilot scheme. Successful developments in the United Kingdom should be examined, such as Shape organisations, but ultimately the success of the new initiative will depend on how closely it is attuned to local circumstances and needs.

11.17 The structure and placing of a new arts and disability development is of the greatest importance and we urge that serious consideration be given as to whether an arts or a disability organisation would provide the most suitable base. The NICH has adequate administrative back-up to support such a development but whether at this stage the arts could be given priority among the many important concerns of that council is a matter for discussion. At any rate, in order for a new organisation to thrive, stable funding and back-up resources are necessary, and we hope that the various statutory and voluntary organisations involved so far will co-operate to establish a shared funding commitment for a three-year development period. In addition to considering the funding needs of the new development we *recommend* that the Arts Council should assist with artistic matters on which the new organisation wishes to evolve policies. After three years the pilot project should be assessed and proposals made for further developments.

Health and personal social services

11.18 We have discussed in Chapter 6 our belief that co-ordination is needed in order to ensure the growth of arts practice in the National Health Service. Taking into account that responsibility for health and personal social services rests with a single body in Northern Ireland, we believe that the most suitably-placed individual within each board to act as co-ordinator is the Liaison Officer for the Voluntary Sector. Often part of headquarters staff, this officer has adequate seniority and ready access to a wide range of organisations representing disabled people. We believe that existing officers have difficulties caused by lack of resources (there are no funds attached to these posts) and therefore *recommend* that funds be found by Area Boards to ensure that the extension of remit which we urge can become effective.

Hospital Advisory Service

11.19 The DHSS Regional Strategic Plan 1983-88[5] proposes the establishment of a Hospital Advisory Service. We hope that such a service will look at innovations in the arts in health service provision and will seek to spread information about examples of good practice to institutions which could benefit. We urge that discussion be initiated between the proposed Hospital Advisory Service and the Liaison Officers for the Voluntary Sector mentioned in paragraph 11.18 so as to develop methods of assessing and presenting for general debate and adoption the most promising initiatives.

Education

11.20 In Northern Ireland, special education services are ordinarily provided by the education and library boards. As a result of the Education Order

1984[6] a new legal framework will come into being which brings the provision of education for children with special needs in Northern Ireland roughly into line with the system which has operated in Great Britain since the Education Act 1981. However, until now, when children have been assessed to be in need of 'special care', responsibility for their education, care and training has passed to the Health and Social Services Boards. Such children do not have a statutory right to these services and it is acknowledged that some, believed to be a relatively small number, for whom these services are appropriate, do not receive them.

11.21 Educational provision for children with severe mental handicap outside the normal education system has been retained in the belief that continuity of life-long care is essential to their development. In addition, existing responsibilities were seen to contribute towards a smooth transition from school to adult training centre, with the parallel development of school and adult training centre programmes providing for continuing educational progress. Despite these advantages, opinion in Northern Ireland has been divided on the desirability of the present system with the Ulster Teachers' Union seeking the immediate transfer of responsibility for the education of mentally handicapped children to the Department of Education.

11.22 In December 1984, following extensive public consultation and three debates in the Northern Ireland Assembly, the Secretary of State for Northern Ireland announced the Government's decision to bring mentally handicapped children into the statutory education system with responsibility for their education being transferred to the Department of Education. Legislation to implement the decision being in hand, the target date for the transfer of responsibility was set at early 1987.

11.23 The planned change in the status of severely mentally handicapped children should eventually do much to reduce the difficulties caused by the present arrangements which include lack of an appropriate training course for intending teachers in special care schools. The provision of more adult training centres will relieve special care schools where, at present, as many as a quarter of the pupils are over 19 years of age. The Department of Health and Social Services states that the arts already play a large part in daily programmes in existing special care schools and we hope that as changes in the status of and responsibility for mentally handicapped children are implemented, this situation will continue to obtain, backed up by initial and in-service teacher training in the arts.

Scotland

Local government and the arts

11.24 The Local Government and Planning (Scotland) Act 1982[7] makes it the duty of district councils in Scotland to 'ensure that there is adequate provision of facilities for the inhabitants of their area for recreational, sporting, cultural and social activities'. District councils are given powers to provide for such activities as well as to contribute towards the expenses incurred by others who do so, such as voluntary organisations or other local authorities.

11.25 The same Act gives to regional councils powers to make financial contributions towards such activities and specifically mentions the promotion of 'music, theatre, opera, ballet and other arts'. This latter phrase was included in the legislation in response to the concern expressed by national and touring arts companies, who feared that without financial support from the regions their survival would be in question; and by the district councils, many of whom objected to being expected to take over the funding of performances which did not directly benefit their own constituents. In addition, many felt that their limited budgets should not be expected to support companies they saw as being a national responsibility and so a proper charge on the funds of central government. The situation for the national and touring companies continues to cause concern, with amalgamation and the sharing of expenses and resources being among the suggested solutions in the Scottish Arts Council's recent report *The Next Five Years*.[8] It should nevertheless be recognised that Scottish local authorities[9] currently spend about 1½ times as much as the Scottish Arts Council on the arts (including museums and galleries).

11.26 So far as initiatives involving disabled people are concerned, while there is no reason to imagine that leisure and recreation departments in district councils have any less sympathy for the needs of disabled people than the regional council departments had, it has in practice been unusual for district councils to support the same volume of arts activity generally as had their predecessors. Many district councils, struggling to maintain essential services, have sacrificed projects which do not cause a public outcry by their disappearance, and among these have been projects in the arts involving disabled people.

11.27 One area of growth is tourism and figures show that three of the top four attractions in Scotland are art galleries and museums.[10] It may be partly because of this that some district councils have appointed arts officers; and some, local arts councils with powers to make recommendations to committees of the district councils, to raise funds and to give grants. This development goes some way towards filling the gap caused by the lack of Regional Arts Associations in Scotland and benefits in particular arts projects with a significant amateur component, into which category many initiatives involving disabled people fall.

11.28 Several district councils now have appointments within their leisure and recreation departments for officers with responsibility for sport and disabled people or for leisure and disabled people. This growing commitment reflects the background work undertaken over a number of years by the Scottish Sports Council, which encouraged the establishment of voluntary regional committees to promote the needs and aspirations of disabled people in sport. The work of these committees, in conjunction with appointed officers, has done much to bring disabled people into the public eye in sporting activities. All seem to have succeeded in raising public awareness of the sporting needs of disabled people with the result that more account is taken of these needs in framing policy. One district council, Aberdeen, has appointed an additional officer with responsibility for disabled people - to work in the arts. We would like to see more of this latter type of development and *recommend* that the Convention of Scottish Local Authorities initiate a meeting to seek ways of increasing the involvement of their members in promoting the arts with disabled people and, in particular, to explore the work of local arts councils and officers in this field.

Access officers and Access panels

11.29 On 4 March 1985, the Building Standards (Scotland) Amendment Regulations 1984[11] will come into effect requiring that there should be access at ground-floor level for disabled people in a wide range of new buildings and in alterations and extensions to the same categories of existing buildings. Although the new regulations go some way towards making provision for disabled people throughout buildings, they will have a minimal effect on most arts facilities, housed in old or new multi-level centres. The task of access officers, appointed in each district council in Scotland, therefore remains largely one of persuasion and encouragement. In this, support comes in an increasing number of districts from local access panels. Panels include members drawn from the voluntary organisations representing disabled people and from the relevant departments of local government as well as individuals who are disabled or who have a particular interest in the question of access. Access panels may undertake access surveys on behalf of other organisations. For example, the Scottish Tourist Board's 1984 publication entitled *Accommodation for Visitors with a Disability*[12] was compiled from information supplied by the Scottish Council on Disability and by local access panels throughout Scotland. Access panels have also been involved with the publication of local access guides or in local advice and information services such as DIAL organisations. We urge that panels carrying out access surveys include arts buildings as a matter of particular concern and recognise that the lack of readily available information about access to the arts is a powerful hindrance to disabled people wishing to participate. We regard the existence of an effective panel as of prime importance in raising awareness of the needs of disabled people and close liaison between access officers and access panels as the essential corollary.

Scottish Arts Council

11.30 The Scottish Arts Council (SAC), although technically a sub-committee of the Arts Council of Great Britain (ACGB), is in practice largely autonomous in its decision making. Like the ACGB, the SAC has recently produced a report outlining its development plans - *The Next Five Years*.[13] This document makes no mention of disabled people.

11.31 However, the Scottish Arts Council has already made a substantial commitment to the development of opportunities for disabled people to be involved in the arts through the provision of revenue funding for the Scottish Committee for Arts and Disability's (SCAD) three- year pilot programme 1980-1983. The period of revenue funding being over, the former SCAD, now established as a full committee of the Scottish Council on Disability entitled the Committee on Arts for Scotland, applies for and receives funds for individual projects in the same way as the SAC's other clients. This situation is unsatisfactory, leaving a number of worthwhile projects without backing.

11.32 The SAC's concern is with the professional arts and applications are assessed on their artistic merits by individual art-form committees. Projects involving disabled people in the arts may, for a variety of reasons, fall outside present funding policies, perhaps through significant amateur involvement. There may be a lack of established artistic criteria by which to judge them, or committee members may lack enough knowledge about disability to enable them to decide whether or not projects are worth supporting. These difficulties, combined with the current lack of a policy towards disabled people within the SAC have, in practice, resulted in applicants and enquirers being referred to the SCD Committee on Arts for Scotland but, at present, it is unclear as to whether this Committee is expected to vet them and return the successful ones to the Scottish Arts Council for further consideration or themselves seek funding for the projects from other sources.

11.33 There is a danger that the SCD Committee on Arts for Scotland is seen as a mini-arts council supporting the arts involving disabled people, when in reality, in common with the rest of the voluntary sector, it must raise any funds it needs to promote ventures on its own. Further, the Committee's activities and expertise by no means extend throughout all the various art forms, in every sort of situation, with all disability groups. In addition, an expectation that the Committee on Arts ought to undertake every sort of activity might tend to discourage *bona fide* organisations with legitimate interests in the arts and disability quite separate from those of the Committee. We note that the SAC is holding discussions with the aim of creating a policy on disabled people and *recommend* that in its discussions a series of priorities for arts funding involving disabled people be devised in consultation with the SCD Committee on Arts for Scotland and other arts and disability organisations in Scotland.

Further, the SAC should clarify its stance on a number of issues including the relative positions of amateur and professional work, whether preferential treatment should be given to integrated provision, how SAC art-form committees can be enabled to draw on outside expertise from this field of work when considering applications, and where the division of responsibilities for funding projects lies between the SAC and the SCD Committee on Arts for Scotland.

SCD Committee on Arts for Scotland

11.34 As a full committee of the Scottish Council on Disability (SCD), the Committee on Arts for Scotland should enjoy the back-up resources available to the SCD, and has a clear responsibility to mirror in its work the national concerns of the Council. As an epilogue to its pilot programme and a prologue to its new development phase we *recommend* that the Committee on Arts draw up a list of short-term and long-term priorities in which all the various aspects of the Scottish Council's work, including access and information, are taken on board in relation to the arts. This task should be undertaken in full consultation with arts organisations and organisations for disabled people. Plans should be made to encourage the creation of autonomous bodies at regional level, who will represent and promote the interests of disabled people in the arts (as Artlink in Edinburgh and the Lothians and Project Ability in Glasgow intend to do in their separate localities) and inform the Committee on Arts about local needs and concerns. Only by regular and full consultation can the Committee effectively represent the needs and aspirations of those it serves to funding bodies, policy makers, central government, training establishments and the media.

11.35 The Committee should, in our view, endeavour to present to statutory bodies examples of good practice through the promotion of model projects and should seek to spread interest in and acceptance of this type of work among policy makers. In the field of training, the Committee should work to raise the awareness of existing training establishments and artists in order to further developments in initial as well as in-service training for professional care and other staff.

11.36 We would like to see a far more significant role played by the Committee on Arts for Scotland's News-sheet. Besides being an information calendar, the news-sheet should provide space for artists to communicate with readers about work they wish to promote, for staff to let readers know of their needs, and for disabled people to tell about their involvement in the arts. In short the news-sheet should provide a platform for the interested community to extend awareness, conduct debate, and express its concerns. Staff time would need to be devoted to this expanded role for the news-sheet, but we believe that unless a strong platform exists, efforts will continue to take place in isolation and their full potential effect never be realised.

The Scottish Hospital Advisory Service

11.37 The Scottish Hospital Advisory Service (SHAS) was instituted in 1970 as a result of public and political concern about conditions in long-stay hospitals. The SHAS seeks to advise and guide health boards on the general management of hospitals, the promotion of good patient care and the environmental conditions of patients. So far, the SHAS has not included the practice of the arts in long-stay hospitals within its purview. We *recommend* that SHAS co-operate with the SCD Committee on Arts for Scotland and the Scottish Arts Council to initiate and assess, after suitable preliminary research, a specific and substantial arts development in a long-stay hospital. Such an initiative would help to raise the general level of awareness about the value of the arts for patients and residents and present the positive prospect of increasing arts practice in institutions in line with accepted standards of excellence.

Arts therapies

11.38 A small number of arts therapists are employed through health board, social work or education departments in Scotland. In particular a team of six music therapists working at a variety of institutions is making a considerable impact on health care in the south east. In the west of Scotland, a conference and a study day on music therapy attracted representatives of many branches of the caring professions and led to the planning of a series of seminars in 1985. A small number of art therapists have sought to encourage interest in art therapy training in the Scottish art colleges, but so far resources have not enabled plans to be formulated. One movement therapist is employed full-time in the health service and from 1983 to 1985 is pioneering a training course in movement therapy with six volunteers who work in related professional fields. Various voluntary and arts organisations organise one-off training events in the arts therapies but full-time professional training courses are available only in England.

Local initiatives

11.39 We have been dismayed to learn that a number of arts and disability initiatives in Scotland are struggling through lack of funds and that valuable developments which flourished in the 1970s are in grave danger of being lost. We have heard from funding agencies that they are finding it so difficult to maintain existing provision that they cannot contemplate new developments and from arts bodies that their work is threatened in both quantity and quality by constraints of funding. However, even in such difficult times, one or two organisations flourish and one such is the Council for Music in Hospitals which, although a comparatively recent entrant into the arts and disability world in Scotland, continues to establish and expand its services in spite of constant worries about fund raising.

11.40 We urge funding bodies to remember that they are part of a very small community of funding agencies in Scotland and when funds are cut from arts work involving disabled people there is often nowhere else to go. And we urge arts organisations, cutting back on activities in order to survive, not to cut work involving disabled people if they can possibly avoid it. Disabled people will need to make their protests heard and their wishes known, in order that services gained at great cost do not disappear.

Education

11.41 The responsibility for providing education locally in Scotland rests mainly with the nine regional councils and three island councils. Except for the universities, general supervision is exercised by the Secretary of State acting through the Scottish Education Department. We *recommend* that the Secretary of State should arrange for the education system to be examined in the light of the principles set out in Chapter 9 of our report with a view to evolving and announcing a policy on the arts education of disabled people in Scotland.

Wales

11.42 The aims we have set out in this report apply to Wales as to the rest of the United Kingdom, but in determining the best means of achieving these aims, some special features of the Welsh scene need to be taken into account.

11.43 Like the Scottish Arts Council, the Welsh Arts Council is technically a sub-committee of the Arts Council of Great Britain but is largely autonomous in its decision-making. The work of the Welsh Arts Council is assisted by three Regional Arts Associations - for North Wales, West Wales and South-East Wales - though the relationship between these Associations and the Welsh Arts Council differs in some respects from that which obtains between the Regional Arts Associations in England and the Arts Council of Great Britain.

11.44 Use of the Welsh language is one important aspect of a specifically Welsh culture in which it is essential that disabled people should be enabled to play their full part. The pattern of arts activity is by no means uniform across the country, and the Welsh-speaking population ranges from less than 10 per cent in the eastern and southern fringes to over 90 per cent in North-Western Wales.

11.45 Disabled people face particular problems in taking part in arts activities in the dispersed rural areas in which about a third of the people of Wales live. Village halls and other meeting places are often difficult for disabled people to get to, and the facilities provided may be ill-adapted to their needs. The three Regional Arts Associations recognise that insufficient is done to make things easier for disabled people but the very limited resources of these Associations are already severely stretched.

11.46 There are eight 'theatre in education/community' tours in Wales, one for each county. They all attempt to include in their programme work for special schools, but this inevitably limits their community work. There is one drama group (HIJINX) which devotes part of its annual programme to a production specifically for audiences of mentally handicapped people. In addition, there is a small number of community arts teams, with a strong commitment to carrying out work with disabled people. There is an acute shortage of qualified art, drama and music therapists, and we understand that there is no arts therapy training agency in Wales.

11.47 There are grounds for thinking that the arts opportunities for disabled people in Wales lag behind those for disabled people elsewhere in the United Kingdom. One response has been the formation of Arts for Disabled People in Wales. This was the result of a seminar held in April 1982 and attended by delegates from the arts community and the disabled community. In November 1982 a full-time Development Officer and part-time Administrator were appointed to co-ordinate and foster arts activities for people with disabilities throughout Wales. The organisation now operates from a small corner of the Caerphilly offices of the Wales Council for the Disabled.

11.48 A report published in 1982 by Arts for Disabled People in Wales, entitled *The First Two Years*, shows the progress that has been made. Among the organisation's current activities is an attempt to secure better integration of entries from disabled young people in the Eisteddfod programme and the programmes of other festivals without standards being compromised. But although an encouraging start has been made, the organisation's resources are much too limited to enable it to match the needs of disabled people in the whole of Wales; and it is clear that for satisfactory results to be achieved far better co-ordination will be needed between the various bodies concerned with increasing arts opportunities.

11.49 The All-Wales Strategy for Development of Services for Mentally Handicapped People already provides one channel for action on our report, and we strongly urge that any strategy which may be devised in relation to other groups of disabled people should build in provision for the arts and arts therapies. More generally, we believe that a thorough reappraisal should now be made of the allocation of resources in Wales for the purpose of helping physically and mentally handicapped people to become more fully involved in arts activities, including, where appropriate, arts therapy. We *recommend* that the Secretary of State for Wales should arrange for such a review to be undertaken, bringing into consultation local authorities and health authorities as well as the Welsh Arts Council, Regional Arts Associations and representatives of voluntary organisations including Arts for Disabled People in Wales.

References

1 Department of Education.
Recreation and Youth Services Order,
Statutory Instrument 961 NI 12. DOE,
Northern Ireland, 1973

2 Department of Education.
Education and Library Order, Statutory
Instrument 1263 NI 12. DOE, Northern
Ireland, 1972

3 Co-operation North.
*Services for Physically Disabled People in
Northern Ireland and the Republic of
Ireland*, Co-operation North, Belfast and
Dublin, 1984

4 Department of the Environment.
Building (Amendment) Regulations NI
1984. HMSO, 1984

5 Department of Health and Social
Services.
*Regional Strategic Plan for the Health and
Personal Social Services in Northern
Ireland, 1983-88*. DHSS, Northern
Ireland, 1983

6 Department of Education.
Education (Northern Ireland) Order,
Statutory Instrument 1136 NI 16. DOE,
Northern Ireland, 1984

7 Local Government Division of the
Scottish Development Department.
*Local Government and Planning
(Scotland) Act 1982*

8 Scottish Arts Council.
The Next Five Years, SAC, Edinburgh,
1984

9 Scottish Arts Council.
*Local Authority Expenditure on the Arts in
the financial year to 31 March 1981*
(Report published annually). SAC,
Edinburgh, 1982

10 Scottish Tourist Board.
Annual Survey of Visitor Attractions 1982,
STB, Edinburgh 1983

11 Buildings Division of the Scottish
Development Department.
*Building Standards (Scotland) Amendment
Regulations 1984, HMSO, 1984*

12 Scottish Tourist Board.
*Accommodation for Visitors with a
Disability in Hotels and Guest-Houses*,
STB, Edinburgh, 1984

13 Scottish Arts Council.
The Next Five Years, SAC Edinburgh,
1984

14 Arts for Disabled People in Wales.
The First Two Years, report available
from Arts for Disabled People in Wales,
Caerbragady Estate, Bedwas Road,
Caerphilly CF8 3SL

Chapter 12

The way ahead

12.1 It will be seen that our proposals centre on certain themes:

(a) Those responsible for arts funding in both the public and private sectors have it in their power to ensure that much better provision is made for disabled people by adapting the conditions on which funds are made available.

(b) In general, the arts needs of disabled people will be best served by working through existing organisations, rather than by attempting to set up some new umbrella-type organisation on a national scale.

(c) Every effort should be made to ensure that disabled people can pursue arts interests alongside other members of the community, but where this is not possible, or where the disabled people themselves prefer it, separate provision should be made.

(d) The present arrangements for getting information to disabled people about arts events and arts facilities are in urgent need of improvement.

(e) Changes made in the interests of disabled people are often found to be of benefit to the community as a whole. Thus buildings adapted to the needs of people with walking difficulties often thereby become safer and easier for others to use. Good visual design is of benefit to those with normal sight as well as to those whose sight is poor.

(f) It is at least as important to ensure that disabled people are enabled and encouraged to participate actively in the arts, whether in paid employment or otherwise, as that they should have better facilities for joining the audience.

(g) The arts have a crucial part to play in education and training so as to develop more constructive public attitudes towards disabled people, and to increase the confidence and expectations of disabled people themselves.

(h) A new framework should be established for use of the arts and arts therapies in the National Health Service and the social services.

(i) Particular efforts should be made by arts and disability organisations to educate their staff, their members and the public in more constructive attitudes to the arts involvement of people with disabilities in accordance with the wishes of such people.

12.2 It did not take us long to decide that the main need was not to identify the barriers to fuller involvement of disabled people in the arts. The barriers were usually clear enough. What had been lacking was a sufficiently comprehensive and resolute attack on these barriers, which involves a change in attitudes as well as, in some instances, a change in physical provision. In addition to preparing our report we have, therefore, devoted our resources to taking the various initiatives described in Chapter 2. We are confident that these initiatives will yield practical results, but inevitably they will be very small in relation to the scale of the need.

12.3 With the submission of this report, our remit as a committee is discharged, but we are glad to know that the Carnegie United Kingdom Trust propose to establish a Carnegie Council and to maintain a small unit for a year or more to monitor progress on the implementation of our recommendations. We have assembled a great deal more information than could be specifically mentioned in this report, and the Council will be able to use some of this in articles and other publications. All the evidence we have received will also be at the disposal of Simon Goodenough who has been commissioned by the Carnegie United Kingdom Trust to write a book on matters relevant to our Inquiry.

12.4 In preparing this report, grammatical neccessity has obliged us to refer to disabled people as 'they'. In some ways it would have been more appropriate to refer to them as 'we'. Not only are some of the members of our own Committee disabled, but we all attach great importance to the fact that disabled people are as much a part of the wider community as able-bodied people.

12.5 One other verbal matter merits comment. In view of our belief that attitudes are at least as important as material provision we think it worthwhile to explain why the word 'discrimination' does not figure prominently in our report. A habit has grown up of referring in a wide variety of circumstances to 'discrimination against' disabled people. This term is apt for situations in which disabled people are deliberately selected for unfavourable treatment, but many of the avoidable disadvantages which disabled people experience in relation to the arts are the result of a failure to recognise and then cater for their particular needs rather than of any deliberate attempt to deny them opportunities which are open to others. To refer to 'discrimination against' disabled people in this wider context, and so imply malevolent design where there has been no more than thoughtlessness, inadvertence, lack of effort, or lack of knowledge, may lead to unnecessary tensions and resentments.

12.6 There has been recent Parliamentary consideration of legislative proposals designed to make it unlawful to 'discriminate unreasonably' against another person on the grounds of disability, and also of proposals for establishing a Commission with functions in the area. By commenting on the use of the word 'discrimination' we must not be taken as stating an attitude on these particular proposals, and still less as registering opposition to the use of legislation to protect the interests of disabled people. There are some instances where all of us are positively in favour of using the law for this purpose, as will be apparent from our comments in Chapter 4 on the provisions of the building regulations.

12.7 All members of our Committee are in total agreement as to the importance of expanding arts opportunities for disabled people, but some of us are more optimistic than others about the possible pace of advance. Our recommendations constitute a minimum programme which should, in the opinion of all of us, be achievable in substantial measure within a very few years, and should also provide a sound basis for further improvement as resources and other circumstances allow.

12.8 Everyone concerned about the arts, and everyone involved in organisations for disabled people, should take an active interest in the issues discussed in this report. Our fervent hope is that those within whose power it lies to expand and improve the arts opportunities of disabled people will rise swiftly to the challenge. This greater recognition of the needs of disabled people will contribute not only to their good, but to the well-being of society as a whole.

Appendix 1

Organisations which have provided evidence

(including, in some cases, oral evidence) other than in regional meetings

The Committee learned a great deal also from points raised at regional meetings and in individual correspondence but it has not been practicable to list all those who helped in this way.

England and Wales

Access and Information Group
Action Space London Events
Age Concern, England
Alyn and Deeside District Council
Area Museum Council for the South West
Area Museums Service for South Eastern England
Artists' General Benevolent Institution
Arts Access
Arts Council of Great Britain
Arts for Disabled People in Wales
Artsline
Association For All Speech Impaired Children
Association for Dance Movement Therapy
Association for Independent Disabled Self Sufficiency
Association of British Theatre Technicians
Association of County Councils
Association of Dance Therapists
Association of Disabled Professionals
Association of District Councils
Association of Professional Music Therapists in Great Britain
Association of Professions for the Mentally Handicapped
Automobile Association
Bath Association for the Disabled
Blyth Valley Council for the Disabled
Bradford DIAL
Brent, London Borough of: Young Disabled Unit
Bristol, University of, Extra-mural Department
British Arts
British Association of Art Therapists
British Association of Dramatherapists
British Association of Social Workers
British Association of Teachers of the Deaf
British Broadcasting Corporation
British Council
British Deaf Association
British Limbless Ex-Service Men's Association
British Medical Association
British Polio Fellowship - Leeds Branch
British Railways Board
British Red Cross Society
British Society for Music Therapy
British Standards Institution
British Theatre Association
Bromley Chain
Buckingham Arts Association
Calvert Trust Adventure Centre for Disabled People
Campaign for Mentally Handicapped People
Carousel
Centre for Policy on Ageing
Centre for Post-graduate Psychiatry, Central Birmingham Health Authority
Children's World
Cinematograph Exhibitors' Association
Clwyd County Council
College of Occupational Therapists
College of Occupational Therapy (Liverpool) Ltd
Committee of Directors of Polytechnics
Community Council of Essex
Conquest
Council for Advancement of Communication with Deaf People
Council for National Academic Awards
Council for the Care of Churches
Crafts Council

Dance for Everyone
Deaf Broadcasting Campaign
Depressives Associated
Derbyshire Association for the Disabled
Disabilities Study Unit
Disabled Drivers' Association
Disabled Living Foundation
Dorset Association for the Disabled
East Hertfordshire Community Health
Council
East Midlands Area Museum Service
East Midlands Arts Association
Eastern Arts Association
English Tourist Board
Equity
Gloucestershire Royal Hospital
Graeae Theatre Company
Greater London Association for Disabled
People
Greater Manchester Youth Association
Greenwich Association of the Disabled
Hertfordshire Association for the
Disabled
Hertfordshire College of Art and Design
Highway Community Arts Project
Historic Buildings and Monuments
Commission - English Heritage
Humberside Society for the Physically
Handicapped
Independent Broadcasting Authority
Independent Theatre Council
Inner London Education Authority
Interface Productions Ltd
Interim Theatre Company
Interlink
Laban Centre for Dance and Movement
Lancashire County Council: County
Advisory Service
Leicester City Council
Library Association
Lincolnshire and Humberside Arts
Lincolnshire County Council
Link: British Centre for Deafened
People
Luton, Recreation Services Committee
Maelor General Hospital, Wrexham
Manchester Hospitals' Arts Project
Manchester Polytechnic
Manchester, City of: Cultural Services
Department
Manpower Services Commission
Meanwood Park Hospital - Continuing
Education Unit, Leeds
MENCAP (see Royal)
Mental Health Film Council

Merseyside Deaf Channel Group
Mid Glamorgan Health Authority
Mobility International
Mouth and Foot Painting Artists
Multiple Sclerosis Society
Muscular Dystrophy Group of Great
Britain and Northern Ireland
Museum and Art Gallery Service for
Yorkshire and Humberside
Museums and Galleries Commission
Museums Association
National Association for Design
Education
National Association for Education in the
Arts
National Association of Swimming Clubs
for the Handicapped
National Association of Teachers in
Further and Higher Education
National Council of Women of Great
Britain
National Deaf Children's Society
National Federation of Gateway Clubs
National Information Forum
National Society for Art Education
National Trust
Nordoff-Robbins Music Therapy Centre
North of England Museums Service
North West Arts
North Western Museum and Art Gallery
Service
Northern Arts
Northwick Park Hospital, Middlesex
Norwich City College of Further and
Higher Education
Nottinghamshire County Council:
Education Department
Open University
Orchard Hill Further Education Unit,
Queen Mary's Hospital, Carshalton
Oxfordshire County Council:
Department of Museum Services
Physically Handicapped and Able
Bodied Group, Whitham
Pilgrim Hospital, Lincolnshire
Rockley Mount School (Barnsley MBC)
Royal British Legion Royal College of
Nursing
Royal College of Psychiatrists
Royal Hospital and Home for Incurables
Royal Institute of British Architects
Royal National Institute for the Blind
Royal National Institute for the Deaf
Royal Society for Mentally Handicapped
Children and Adults (MENCAP)

Shape Services
Shelton Trust Ltd
Soundpost Musical Instrument Co-
  operative
South East Arts Association
South West Arts Association
Southampton Art Gallery
Southern Arts Association
Souvenir Press
Spastics Society
Springfield Hospital
Standing Conference of Women's
  Organisations
Tatchbury Mount Hospital,
  Southampton
Thamesdown, Borough of, Arts and
  Recreation Department
Trades Union Congress
Volunteer Centre
Wales: North, West and South East
  Regional Arts Associations
Wales College of Librarianship
Wales Council for the Deaf
Walsgrave Hospital, Coventry
Waverley Borough Council
West Midlands Area Museum Service
West Midlands Arts Association
West Midlands County Council
Winged Fellowship Trust
Worcestershire Association for Disabled
  People
Yorkshire Arts Association
Youth and Music

Northern Ireland and Scotland

Aberdeen, City of - District Council: Art
  Gallery and Museums Department
Age Concern, Scotland
Argyll & Bute District Council:
  Tourism, Leisure & Recreation
Argyll and Clyde Health Board: Renfrew
  District: Merchiston Hospital
Association for Recurrent Education
  (Northern Ireland): Educational
  Guidance Service for Adults
Barnado's, Edinburgh
Bearsden and Milngavie Arts Guild
Berwickshire District Council
Borders Regional Council: Social Work:
  Day Care Centre
Chest, Heart and Stroke Association:
  Volunteer Stroke Scheme

Citizens' Theatre, Glasgow
Clydebank District Council: Technical
  Services
Community Service Volunteers,
  Edinburgh
Convention of Scottish Local Authorities
Council for Museums and Galleries in
  Scotland
Council for Music in Hospitals, Scottish
  Branch
Craigie College of Education, Ayr
Cumbernauld Theatre
Dumfries and Galloway Health Board
Dumfries and Galloway Regional
  Council:
  Social Work: Education: Further
  Education: Physical Planning
Dudhope Arts Centre, Dundee
Dundee, City of - District Council:
  Technical Services
Dunfermline District Council: Technical
  Services
East Kilbride Arts Council
East Kilbride District Council:
  Recreation and Leisure Services
Eden Court Theatre, Inverness
Edinburgh, City of - District Council:
  Recreation: Technical Services:
  Theatres and Halls
Edinburgh District Local Health Council
Edinburgh Festival Fringe Society
Edinburgh International Festival
Educational Institute of Scotland
Epilepsy Association of Scotland
Fair Play for Children in Scotland
Fife Health Board: East Fife District:
  Cameron Hospital
Fife Regional Council: Education
Glasgow, City of - District Council:
  Parks and Recreation
Gordon District Council: Administration
Grampian Regional Council: Special
  Education
Highland Health Board: Southern
  District
Highlands and Islands Development
  Board
Institute of Leisure and Amenity
  Management, Scotland Region
Inverness Access Committee
Irvine Development Corporation
Kincardine and Deeside District
  Council: Environmental Health
Lothian Health Board

Lothian Regional Council: Community Education
MacRobert Arts Centre, Stirling
Mental Welfare Commission for Scotland
Monklands District Council: Leisure and Recreation
Moray District Council: Housing and Technical Services
Moray House College of Education, Edinburgh
Motherwell District Council: Technical Services
Mull Little Theatre
National Association of Youth Orchestras, Edinburgh
National Gallery of Scotland
National Museum of Antiquities of Scotland
Nithsdale District Council: Parks and Recreation
Northern Ireland Council for the Handicapped
Northern Ireland Office: Department of Education
Orkney Islands Council: Education: Community Education
Perth and Kinross District Council: Environmental Health
Physically Handicapped and Able Bodied (PHAB), Perth
Pier Arts Centre, Orkney
Queen Margaret College, Edinburgh: Occupational Therapy
Randalstown and Antrim Physically Handicapped Action Group, Northern Ireland
Royal Scottish Academy of Music and Drama
Saltire Society, Edinburgh
Scottish Association of Youth Clubs: Orkney: Lerwick
Scottish Arts Council
Scottish Centre for the Tuition of the Disabled
Scottish Committee for Arts and Disability
Scottish Committee on Access for Disabled People
Scottish Conservative Party
Scottish Education Department
Scottish Further Education Association
Scottish Library Association
Scottish National Party

Scottish Office: Department of the Environment: Property Services Agency: Social Work Services Group
Scottish Society for the Mentally Handicapped: Glasgow: Montrose and District: Dumfries and District: Buckie Branch
Scottish Spina Bifida Association
Scottish Sports Council
Scottish Standing Conference of Voluntary Youth Organisations
Scottish Tourist Board
Scottish Women's Rural Institutes
Shetland Islands Council: Leisure and Recreation Department
Shetland Islands Council: Social Work
Social Democratic Party, Edinburgh
St Josephs Hospital, Midlothian: Consultant Psychiatrist: Nurse Tutor: Drama Worker with the Handicapped
Stirling District Arts Council
Stirling District Council: Leisure and Recreation: Planning and Building Control
Strathclyde Fire Brigade
Strathclyde Regional Council: Education: Argyll & Bute: Ayr: Dunbarton: Glasgow: Lanark: Renfrew: Community Education: Glasgow: Lanark: Renfrew: Ayr: Bearsden & Milngavie: Cumbernauld & Kilsyth: Dumbarton: Clydebank: Strathkelvin: East Kilbride: Social Work
STV, Scottish Television plc
Tayside Regional Council: Social Work: Education
Theatre Royal, Glasgow
Ulster Hall, Belfast

Appendix 2

Addresses of some link organisations

Arts Councils

Arts Council of Great Britain
105 Piccadilly,
London W1V 0AU
Tel: 01 629 9495

Arts Council of Northern Ireland
181a Stranmillis Road
Belfast BT9 5DU
Tel: 0232 663591

Scottish Arts Council
19 Charlotte Square
Edinburgh EH2 4DF
Tel: 031 226 6051

Welsh Arts Council
Holst House, 9 Museum Place
Cardiff CF1 3NX
Tel: 0002 394711

Regional Arts Associations

Council of Regional Arts Associations
39 St James's Street
London SW1A 1LL
Tel: 01 629 9586

East Midlands Arts Association
Mountfields House, Forest Road
Loughborough, Leicester LE11 3HU
Tel: 0509 218292

Eastern Arts Association
8/9 Bridge Street
Cambridge CB2 1UA
Tel: 0223 357596

Greater London Arts Association
25-31 Tavistock Place
London WC1H 9SF
Tel: 01 388 2211

Lincolnshire and Humberside Arts
St Hugh's, Newport
Lincoln LN1 3DN
Tel: 0522 33005

Merseyside Arts
Bluecoat Chambers, School Lane
Liverpool L1 3BX
Tel: 051 709 0671

Mid-Pennine Arts Association
2 Hammerton Street
Burnley, Lancashire BB11 1NA
Tel: 0282 21986

North Wales Arts Association
10 Wellfield House, Bangor
Gwynedd LL57 1ER
Tel: 0248 353248

North West Arts
4th Floor, 12 Harter Street
Manchester M1 6HY
Tel: 061 228 3062

Northern Arts
10 Osborne Terrace, Jesmond
Newcastle upon Tyne NE2 1NZ
Tel: 0632 816334

South East Arts
9-10 Crescent Road
Tunbridge Wells, Kent TN1 2LU
Tel: 0892 41666

South West Arts
23 Southernhay East, Exeter
Devon EX1 1QG
Tel: 0392 38924

South West Wales Arts Association
Victoria Street, Cwmbran
Gwent NP44 3YT
Tel: 06003 67530/68430

Southern Arts Association
19 Southgate Street, Winchester
Hants SO23 9DQ
Tel: 0962 55099

West Midlands Arts
Brunswick Terrace
Stafford ST16 1BZ
Tel: 0785 59231

West Wales Association for the Arts
Dark Gate, Red Street
Carmarthen Dyfed
Tel: 0267 234248

Yorkshire Arts Association
Glyde House, Glydegate
Bradford, Yorkshire BD5 0BQ
Tel: 0274 723051

Arts Organisations

Shape and Interlink

SHAPE and ARTLINK services are registered charities which link artists and arts companies with organisations and institutions for the disabled and disadvantaged. INTERLINK is the international counterpart with the magazine *Positif*.

SHAPE
9 Fitzroy Square
London W1P 6AE
Tel: 01 388 9744/9622

Art Link (West Midlands)
12 Homesford Terrace, North Street
Newcastle Under Lyme
Tel: 0782 614170

Artlink for Lincolnshire and Humberside
84 Marlborough Avenue
Hull HU5 3JT
Tel: 0482 46012

Artlink - Shape in Oxfordshire and Berkshire
The Studio, 81 Langley Close
Oxford
Tel: 0865 750163/750025

Artshare South West
c/o South West Arts
23 Southernhay East, Exeter
Devon EX1 1QG
Tel: 0392 38924

East Midlands Shape
New Farm, Walton by Kimcote
Lutterworth, Leicestershire LE17 5RL
Tel: 04005 3882

Northern Shape
18/20 Dean Street
Newcastle upon Tyne NE1 1PG
Tel: 0632 612156

North West Shape
21 Whalley Road, Whalley Range
Manchester M168AD
Tel: 061 226 9120

Shape Up North
191 Bellevue Road
Leeds 3
Tel: 0532 431005/6

Scottish Council on Disability Committee on Arts for Scotland
Princes House, 5 Shandwick Place
Edinburgh EH2 4RG
Tel: 031 229 8632

Artlink Edinburgh and the Lothians
4a Forth Street
Edinburgh EH1 3LD
Tel: 031 556 6350

Arts for Disabled People in Wales
Caerbragady Estate, Bedwas Road
Caerphilly Mid-Glamorgan
Tel: 0002 887388

INTERLINK
358 Strand
London WC2R 0HS
Tel: 01 836 5819

Other

Arts Access
c/o GLAD (Greater London Association for the Disabled)
1 Thorpe Close
London W10 5XL
Tel: 01 960 5799

Association for Business Sponsorship for the Arts
12 Abbey Churchyard
Bath BA1 1LY
Tel: 0225 63762

British Film Institute
127 Charing Cross Road
London WC2H 0EA
Tel: 01 437 4355

Crafts Council
12 Waterloo Place
London SW1Y 4AU
Tel: 01 930 4811

Library Association
7 Ridgmount Street
London WC1E 7AE
Tel: 01 636 7543

Museums Association
34 Bloomsbury Way
London WC1A 2SF
Tel: 01 404 4767

Intermediary Councils for Disability

Centre on the Environment for the Handicapped
126 Albert Street
London NW1 7NF
Tel: 01 482 2247

Dial UK
Dial House, 117 High Street
Clay Cross, Chesterfield
Derbyshire S45 9DZ
Tel: 0246 864498

Disabled Living Foundation
380-384 Harrow Road
London W9 2HU
Tel: 01 289 6001

National Bureau for Handicapped Students
40 Brunswick Square
London WC1N 1AZ
Tel: 01 278 3459

Northern Ireland Council for the Handicapped
2 Annadale Avenue
Belfast BT7 3JH
Tel: 0232 640011

PHAB (Physically Handicapped and Able Bodied)
Tavistock House North
Tavistock Square
London WC1H 9HX
Tel: 01 388 1963

Royal Association for Disability and Rehabilitation
25 Mortimer Street
London W1N 8AB
Tel: 01 637 5400

Scottish Council on Disability
Princes House, 5 Shandwick Place
Edinburgh EA2 4RG
Tel: 031 229 8632

Wales Council for the Disabled
Caerbradgy Industrial Estate
Bedwas Road
Caerphilly CF8 3SL
Tel: 0002 887325

Reference books for further information include:

Arts Address Book
ISBN: 0 9504211 46
Peter Marcan
31 Rowliff Road
High Wycombe, Bucks HP12 3LD

Arts Centres, Facilities and Amenities for the Handicapped
ISBN: 0 900270 241
Royal Association for Disability and Rehabilitation
25 Mortimer Street
London W1N 8AB

British Alternative Theatre Directory
ISBN: 0 903931 49 4
John Offord Publications Ltd
PO Box 64
Eastbourne BN21 3LW

British Music Education Yearbook
ISBN: 0 946890 02 1
Rhinegold Publishing Ltd
52a Floral Street
London WC2 E9DA

Directory of Arts Centres 2
ISBN: 0 903931 34 6
John Offord Publications Ltd

Directory for the Disabled
ISBN: 0 85941 1842
Woodhead-Faulkner
(Publishers) Ltd
17 Market Street
Cambridge CB2 3PA

Directory of Grant-Making Trusts
ISBN: 0 904757 15 3
Charities Aid Foundation
48 Pembury Road
Tonbridge, Kent TN9 2DJ

Education Year Book
ISBN: 0 582 90401 3
Longman Group Ltd
Westgate House, Harlow
Essex CM20 1NE

Social Services Year Book
ISBN: 0 582 90403 X
Longman Group Ltd

Grant Making Trusts and Organisations in Scotland
ISBN: 0 903 589 605
Scottish Council of Community and
Voluntary Organisations
19 Claremont Crescent
Edinburgh EH7 4QD

Municipal Year Book
ISBN: 0 900552 37 9
Municipal Publications Ltd
178-202 Great Portland Street
London W1N 6NH

Museums Yearbook
ISBN: 0 902102 59 1
Museums Association
34 Bloomsbury Way
London WC1A 2SF

The Scottish Companion
ISBN: 0 946724 11 3
Carrick Publishing
28 Miller Road
Ayr KA7 2AY

Appendix 3

Regional consultative meetings

In the course of the Inquiry the Committee held 16 consultative meetings - 14 in England and Wales, one in Scotland and one in Northern Ireland. Invitations were sent to a wide range of statutory and non-statutory organisations as well as to individuals who had responded to publicity about the Committee's work. In all about 1,500 people attended these meetings.

The object was to bring together representatives of arts consumers and providers, and of organisations for disabled people, as well as individuals concerned about the arts or about disability. The meetings gave those attending an opportunity to highlight matters for the Committee's attention, to identify innovative work, and to suggest means by which further arts opportunities could be provided for disabled people.

The value of the meetings for individuals depended partly on how familiar they already were with the subject matter of the Inquiry. The wide range of interest groups and experience represented ensured that attention was drawn to many different issues of concern. Specialisation was difficult but some people became more aware of the needs of people with different types of handicap, and others were introduced for the first time to their local arts providers or to hitherto unknown sources of information and help.

This crucial mix of interest groups was the unique feature. For the first time, by bringing together at a regional level the numerous components concerned with the arts and/or disability, the isolation of specialist groups was challenged, and the public's stereotyped images of 'disability', 'art' and 'health' questioned.

Examples of further developments are the Social Services Director meeting his county's Music Adviser for the first time; the offer of the use after hours by the local hospital of the local authority adapted bus; and the adoption by other theatres of a local idea for a script-loaning scheme for people with impaired hearing. A number of other initiatives are known to have come about as a direct result of these meetings.

Interest groups represented

(a) Disabled people

Many local voluntary organisations do not have paid staff and, as the meetings were held during the week, it was not always possible for a representative to attend. Regrettably, a number of these organisations made no response to the invitation or to the invitation to make written comments. It is understandable that disability organisations should be preoccupied with other issues such as benefits, education, employment and welfare services; but it does seem that there is a lack of attention to arts activities.

The most vocal representatives at meetings tended to be those representing physical handicap. The needs of mentally handicapped people, especially those in institutions, were often represented only by the few artists working closely with them in long-stay hospitals or residential settings. On some occasions it was evident that among the needs being overlooked were those of people with visual or hidden handicaps, mental illness or disabilities related to ageing. This perhaps reflected the public's tendency to equate the wheelchair with disability and underlined the danger of assuming that a representative of a disability group would necessarily be alive to the needs of people with handicaps of which he or she had had no direct experience.

(b) Health authorities

District and regional health authorities, when represented, usually sent nurses or occupational therapists. While their commitment to patient care was unquestioned, they often appeared to be fearful of expressing opinions in public and did not hold a sufficiently senior position to recommend and implement necessary changes within their authority. General practitioners were hardly ever present. There was also a lack of health authority members and senior administrative staff. Where they did attend, it was because of an existing commitment to increasing the arts input for their patients.

(c) Arts agencies

The number of art forms and art venues represented varied from meeting to meeting but the range was usually broad and included theatre managers, museum curators, librarians, Regional Arts Association panel members, artists, and amateur and professional organisations.

Few of the arts administrators attending were content with what they were at present doing to encourage participation by disabled people. They saw the meeting as a useful way of developing closer contacts, especially with disability organisations, and identifying what needs there were and how they could best be met, within their very limited budgets.

Many arts administrators admitted that there was a tendency to respond to the demands of those who urged their interest group's needs most strongly, and pointed to the fact that disabled people often failed to lobby. They asked for more help and advice in ensuring that they were meeting the needs of disabled members of the public.

(d) Other agencies

The following were also represented:

(i) Government departments;

(ii) Local authority members and officials with arts responsibilities, or with responsibility for social services, education or planning policies;

(iii) Community Health Councils;

(iv) Regional representatives of national disability and national arts organisations;

(v) Transport, licensing and fire authorities;

(vi) Local newspapers, magazines, television and radio;

(vii) Educational bodies;

(viii) Professional organisations;

(ix) Employment organisations, including the Manpower Services Commission.

The meetings varied in format, but usually began with short talks from three or four local people who had relevant experience but were not necessarily 'experts' in disability. The speakers included a museum curator, a health authority administrator, a special education teacher and a representative of a local disability organisation. The speakers would highlight some of the issues they considered should be tackled. This was followed by discussion, usually in smaller groups, on such matters as:

(i) Funding policies and methods of bringing more arts provision within the reach of people with disabilities;

(ii) Educational facilities;

(iii) Provision for people who are house-bound or in institutions;

(iv) Training of professional and voluntary workers in the arts or in the caring professions;

(v) Arts employment opportunities for disabled people;

(vi) Co-ordination of available services and information and possible means of widening them;

(vii) Access to arts buildings (including provision of equipment and services);

(viii) Media presentation;

(ix) Action to be taken locally as a result of the meeting.

The separate report of these meetings set out the main issues raised and the recommendations that emerged. These recommendations have been taken into account by the Committee in its report.

Carolyn Keen

Appendix 4

Survey of arts publicity material

The availability of accurate information is an essential factor in enabling people with disabilities to participate more fully in arts activities. From information and letters received during the Committee of Inquiry's general investigations, the opinion was formed that, all too often, the information that would enable people with disabilities to get to and use arts venues successfully is not being provided in either publicity material or information guides.

The Committee decided to test this opinion by analysing the information published on arts activities in Eastbourne, Exeter, Hamilton, Leicester, Llandudno, Middlesborough and Winchester, taking particular note of information of use to people with either a mobility or sensory handicap.

The following types of information were examined:

(a) local access guides produced specifically for disabled people;

(b) guides, handbills, etc, issued by the arts venue itself;

(c) guides, 'What's On' etc produced by other organisations or commercial companies such as Tourist Boards and Regional Arts Associations.

The surveys were undertaken by Marks and Spencer management trainees using a survey form designed with the help of the Survey Research Unit, Polytechnic of North London.

171 items of literature were analysed ranging from 35 general guides and 17 access guide entries along with 12 newspaper advertisements, to 16 event posters and 18 venue calendars of events.

The venues covered were theatres, cinemas, arts centres, concert halls, museums, galleries, main reference libraries, churches/ cathedrals, historic buildings and those listed as 'other', eg church halls, civic centres and educational buildings. In fact, 28 per cent of venues fell into the 'other' category demonstrating that the arts take place in a wide range of venues.

As expected, there were very few instances where detailed information relating specifically to a disability was given, for example:

• only 7.1 per cent of the material analysed gave the number of steps at the entrance;

• only 5.4 per cent of the material analysed stated that there was a handrail at the entrance;

• only 3.0 per cent of the material analysed stated that there was a ramped entrance.

When such information was given, it was in an access guide, specifically compiled for disabled people.

While 1.2 per cent of the literature stated that there was a leaflet available giving information of use to people with disabilities, only 17 per cent of all the literature examined stated that there were facilities for disabled people. No event posters, or entries in Regional Arts Association or Local Authority calendars of events or Tourist Board guides, stated whether or not there were facilities for disabled people.

It is particularly disappointing that posters, aimed specifically one assumes at catching the eye, failed to state whether facilities were available or not.

One cannot assume that those venues which did not state that there were facilities did not have them, and only 1.2 per cent of the information analysed stated that the venues were not suitable for disabled people. Only 1 out of 12 booking forms examined stated that there were facilities for wheelchair users. Yet this is vital information for any wheelchair user wishing to book a seat.

None of the five theatres with induction loops carried this information in their booking forms.

Attention was also given to the use of symbols or letters to denote the provision of facilities. This method is sometimes used to reduce the amount of space that would be taken up by writing the information. The wheelchair symbol was used nine times (5.3 per cent) in a wide spread of types of information. The symbols indicating facilities for deaf and visually handicapped people occurred 1.8 per cent and 0.6 per cent times respectively.

Even the basic information of the venue address and telephone number was not included in all cases. This is a further indication that information presentation and content is not considered carefully enough, particularly in relation to disabled people.

Conclusions

The survey suggests that very little of use to disabled people is contained in arts information. Even basic statements, such as 'facilities for disabled people exist', occur infrequently, even though such wording would encourage disabled people to come and take part. Specialist publications, such as access guides, only rarely carry information on arts venues. Improved general information would be of benefit to all arts patrons but especially to disabled people.

Carolyn Keen

Appendix 5

Survey of access facilities

at main arts venues in Edinburgh

Because of the involvement of the Secretary in the Scottish Committee for Arts and Disability it was agreed to undertake a survey of arts venues in the City of Edinburgh, which each year hosts an International Arts Festival. There was also a desire to encourage and form a new Artlink in the region and to use the survey as the basis of a pilot arts information and escort service with disabled people.

The survey was carried out during 1983/84 at the main 30 arts venues in the city by Valerie Nimmo and Teresa Wallace, who had experience of voluntary work and the arts and were keen to develop and widen the Artlink concept to include the services of volunteers. The most important effects of the survey resulted from their contact with and subsequent encouragement to managers of venues about essential improvements, and also from their links with the local access committee and related agencies to make them aware of facilities and obstacles at the arts venues.

Several improvements have resulted from these contacts, in particular from advice at the planning stage of conversion work at the Gallery of Modern Art, the Assembly Rooms and the King's Theatre.

Edinburgh has many historic buildings and steps and stairs. It is a colossal task to create full accessibility to cinemas, theatres, galleries and museums yet there is heartening progress where managements are co-operative. The managers of premises under the control of the City Council had naturally made more progress than owners of commercial buildings such as cinemas and art galleries.

The most difficult appear to be the cinemas owned as part of a national chain, where precedent is often an obstacle to change. Yet the Filmhouse owned by a charitable trust and operated commercially in a converted church has installed induction loop systems for the hard of hearing and now proposes to incorporate a permanent access ramp and toilet facilities despite the burden of funding. The Lyceum Theatre and the City Arts Centre, owned and operated by the City Council have made great strides to provide full accessibility.

However, other factors leave much room for improvement. Only two of the venues had an available public telephone at the BSI recommended height. Suprisingly, British Telecom in Scotland refuses to advise venue owners of the BSI requirements unless asked, and does not advise its engineers to insist on this standard, which seems to be a negative rather than positive attitude to the problem.

Only 13 of the venues had ramped or level entrances; the two main libraries and a major museum had no provision. Only eight venues were fortunate enough to have adapted pavements near to their entrances and car parking varied from impossible to difficult at most venues. Neither the two main libraries nor any cinema and none of the eight main arts centres had negotiated any special parking arrangements with the appropriate authority. The Queen's Hall, a concert hall adapted from a former church, had made an excellent attempt to provide access for wheelchair users, but this was at the rear and the narrow slope for car parking was unsuitable. However the courtesy, co-operation and advisory service of staff overcame many problems.

Inside those centres with the facility of a restaurant or bar, there was access to only eight, and it was suprising how few centres provided even a chair for an ambulant disabled person to rest. Even worse was the fact that only seven venues, not including a cinema, had toilets suitable for all disabled visitors.

The loop-hearing system for the hard of hearing was installed in one cinema, the Rank Odeon, for all three of its studios but was only operative in one at a time, and was not advertised. It was well installed and used in the Filmhouse, and has recently been installed in the Royal Lyceum Theatre and the Playhouse. There is great scope for the improvement of this service for deaf people at little cost. More promising was the admittance of guide dogs with a blind person to 18 of the venues.

There are no facilities for disabled people in the most recent government-funded museum gallery, although the new Gallery of Modern Art has good facilities in a fine converted building. The Royal Scottish Museum also has good facilities in an old building but refuses to operate the National Key Scheme for the control and opening of toilets, which seems a restrictive attitude given other constructive achievements.

There was a noticeable absence of signs and venue-produced publicity to indicate the presence of facilities. The worst example was the case of the major art gallery which did not announce in publicity the availability of wheelchair access and had not replaced its one external sign since its disappearance seven years ago, although this has now been rectified.

Of the 6 theatres, 2 libraries, 5 art galleries, 4 concert halls, 3 museums, 5 cinemas and 5 arts centres surveyed only 6 could be described as reasonably satisfactory overall. These comments are not given as cold criticism because the difficulties of adapting buildings are recognised, but rather to indicate the scope and challenge for further improvement. A similar situation probably appertains in most cities in the United Kingdom.

One recent incident shows the difficulties and the need for constant attention. At a recent charity event in aid of blind welfare held at the main council-managed concert hall, the Usher Hall, the available spaces for wheelchair users were reduced without any consultation from six to two despite encouragement to disabled people to attend.

The information gathered, and the contacts and relationships made with venue managers and other officials, are now being put to good use with the establishment of Artlink Edinburgh and the Lothians. Artlink will follow the pattern of similar services in England but with the important addition of a voluntary information and personal escort service for disabled people to any of the arts venues.

Geoffrey Lord

Artlink Edinburgh and the Lothians is based at:
4 Forth Street, Edinburgh
Tel: 031 556 6350

Appendix 6

Please touch

An evaluative study of a tactile exhibition of sculpture at the British Museum

Perceiving by touch is a fundamental means of experience for everyone, but for those with a visual handicap it may have to take the place of eyesight. Tactile exhibitions for those with a visual handicap - and the attendant problems of signposting, design of labels, security, safeguards against accidental damage, etc - have been mounted both in Britain and abroad. Sometimes they have been documented, but useful information to guide a gallery or an exhibition designer is scarce and scattered.

As part of the evidence gathered by the Committee of Inquiry, it seemed useful to evaluate the 'Please Touch' exhibition put on by the British Museum in 1983, which was open to sighted people as well as those with a visual handicap:-

(a) to give guidance for other galleries and museums;

(b) to document and assess some of the problems encountered and dealt with by the exhibition organisers and designers;

(c) to draw conclusions regarding the future provision of tactile exhibitions open to those with a visual handicap.

The evaluation was started towards the end of the exhibition, so that some of the opinions and reactions of visitors had to be assessed from questionnaires sent out to those who had left their addresses. *Ideally, this kind of evaluation should be considered from the outset.*

In chronological order, these are some of the issues which needed to be resolved:

(1) Conservation objections to extensive handling

(2) Selection of suitable objects

(3) Exhibition design -
lettering design
lighting
layout of exhibits
security of smaller objects
design of labels (braille & large print)
design of signposting (to & within exhibition)
design of a large-print illustrated catalogue
design of a braille catalogue
preparation of a tape-recorded commentary
style of portable tape recorder used
availability of volunteer staff

(4) Advance publicity on a small budget -
informing all clubs and societies for visually handicapped people
radio, television and press advertising
other sources.

'Please Touch' made many innovations, scored many successes, suffered a few setbacks and made some minor mistakes. The evaluation study takes the issues enumerated above and attempts to (a) assess the rationale behind the decisions that were made, (b) determine how successful the decisions were and (c) make positive recommendations for the future.

Positive features of 'Please Touch' included the overall design, and in particular the graphics for signposting and labels, lighting, large-print catalogue, braille catalogue and labels, recorded commentary, length and style of written labels, access to toilet facilities, provision of seating and of volunteer helpers.

Lessons were learned regarding the choice of objects for touching by blind persons. For example, large objects with expanses of homogeneous texture are very difficult to perceive by touch alone.

Delicately textured or carved objects (especially in jade or other smooth material) may be particularly satisfying. Brittle or fragile objects can be handled safely, but require good surveillance by staff and some precautions to prevent theft or accidental dropping. Recorded commentaries are useful and desirable but careful attention needs to be paid to the length of the commentary and the design of the tape player.

Museums and galleries can do a great deal to encourage those with a visual handicap (young and old) to enjoy cultural facilities which they are often denied for trivial reasons. 'Please Touch' (and other tactile exhibitions in Britain and abroad) has shown that *common sense and good design, coupled with adequate publicity* can make a potentially mystifying exhibition clear, safe and rewarding for all but the most severely disabled visitor. Poor eyesight is much more common than blindness and more common than we may think. As with any good design, consideration of the needs of those with a visual handicap can often help the general public and need not conflict with 'aesthetic considerations'.

The evaluation of 'Please Touch' has highlighted some of these issues and drawn attention to others, pointing to the *need for a more coherent, informed approach to the design of exhibitions* of all kinds for those with disabilities. Importantly, the tactile exhibitions and this study go some way to inform the public that 'disability' does not necessarily mean someone in a wheelchair.

The 'Please Touch' experience also suggested that *those with a visual handicap have very low expectations* of the range of cultural facilities they will be able to enjoy. Any organisation which does provide for those with a visual handicap should not only pay extra attention to advance publicity, but should not be disappointed if, at first, attendance by those with a visual handicap appears disappointing - the vicious circle has to be broken somewhere.

Peter Coles

Note:

Copies of the full report 'Please Touch' can be ordered from the Carnegie UK Trust Office, Comely Park House, Dunfermline, Fife. Tel: 0383 721445

Appendix 7

Guidance for funding organisations and applicants on arts projects involving disabled people

Among the basic issues with which the Committee of Inquiry found itself confronted was this : If arts activity is of value to people suffering from one or more disabilities, which arts, which sponsoring or arts organisations, and which projects should be supported, and how should an application for funds, and the value of the ensuing work, be assessed?

The assessment of quality in any activity is difficult enough because an element of subjectivity is almost bound to enter into the process. In the world of the arts, assessment is an age-old issue since every work of art is original and public judgement, and indeed expert opinion, has sometimes failed to divine true creativity or the direction in which an art may be evolving.

When it comes to relating arts activity to a particular section of the community, such as those with a disability, the problem becomes even more difficult. Another level of judgement has to enter. There is that equally important question: is the activity actually beneficial to those involved? Again the answer is certain to be subjective.

The Committee of Inquiry thus asked two of its members as well as five others, including myself, to look at this issue. All of us have had experience enough to be convinced that the arts, in one form or another, can do much to enrich the lives of people who suffer from a major disability and thus be therapeutic in the widest sense of that word, as indeed they are for humanity as a whole. And yet all of us were aware that there can be serious pitfalls however well-intentioned the effort; not only must the activity itself be of a high artistic standard but it must be appropriately devised for its particular purpose and context. There have been negative as well as positive results in this field of endeavour.

From the beginning the group saw the need to enlarge its terms of reference. Much of the work relating the arts to disability so far supported has been financed by the major charitable trusts with strong artistic and educational traditions. While such foundations might well value our findings, they already have much of the expertise they require within their own organisations. The most urgent need to our mind was to encourage other organisations, both in the private and public sectors, to enter the field and thus increase substantially the volume of work going on, enabling it to become part of the country's permanent provision.

The guidelines which have now emerged and which the Committee of Inquiry is publishing separately thus attempt to do two things: first, to outline the great variety of work which receives and awaits further support and, second, to suggest some of the considerations which should be given to applications for funding.

The diversity of work is almost unlimited. It may involve particular disabilities, such as provision for the blind or partially sighted or for the deaf or hard of hearing. It may be concerned with providing better access for the physically disabled to enjoy live theatre, concerts and exhibitions on equal terms with the rest of the community. At the other end of the spectrum provision has to be made for taking art and artists into residential and other centres where the intended beneficiaries are not in a position to share in the normal life of the community.

Initiatives may come from different sources: organisations concerned to bring the arts into touch with the people for whom they are responsible; organisations specifically created, such as 'Shape', to make a bridge between the arts and those with disabilities; and artists and arts organisations anxious to serve particular sections of the disabled community, and among these there may be disabled people themselves.

Without spending too much time on the obvious, the report tries to draw the attention of grant-giving bodies to the sources of advice which it may seem wise to seek when devising policy or assessing applications. The report then goes on to outline what the authors believe to be the aspirations of artists anxious to work in this field, the difficult financial conditions under which many operate, and the kind of experience and aptitudes they should be bringing to the work for which they are seeking support. It is important that the limited financial resources available should be wisely spent, if only to encourage continuity and an increasing measure of support. Activity which fails artistically, or is inappropriate to its context, is inevitably counter-productive in the long run.

The difference between the three categories - project, capital and revenue funding - is also discussed. The first makes all sorts of work possible, encouraging organisations and artists to try out new approaches and schemes of work, often crossing boundaries in terms of both the arts and in categories of disability or adminstration. For the funding organisations this form has the advantage of limited commitment and responsibility. Success can be rewarded with further funding for a limited period and if the project fails to achieve a sufficient measure of success, it can be terminated without embarrassment. The same applies to capital grants, for the purchase of vehicles or lighting, office and other equipment.

The importance of revenue funding is strongly emphasised. The building up of a regular service implies continuing institutional concern, whether this involves the bringing of art and artists into touch with people, or the production of art and teaching services by artists themselves. Organisational overheads such as salaries, travelling and office expenses and telephone, have to be met and this cannot be done properly on the basis of project funding. It is in this field that the public sector has such an important part to play, through the health, education and social service authorities and through the Arts Council of Great Britain, the Crafts Council, the British Film Institute and particularly, the Regional Arts Associations.

The considerations applied to revenue funding are clearly different from those applied to projects, but in both cases the need for building educative relationships between arts organisations and artists on the one hand, and administrators, medical practitioners, nurses and professional therapists on the other, is stressed. Only by this means can joint endeavour and a common language be established. This also extends to the need to train volunteers to support professional work in the arts. The report particularly urges funding organisations to provide separate funds for recording and assessing work, preferably by third parties who combine expertise with independent judgement; such people can provide an important element of energy and support for a worthwhile project.

The report provides lists of Shape services in the UK, of therapy organisations and of arts and disability organisations.

Peter Cox

Chairman of the Group

Note:

Copies of the full report 'Guidance for Funding Organisations and Applicants on Arts Projects involving Disabled People' may be ordered from the Carnegie UK Trust, Comely Park House, Dunfermline, Fife.
Tel: 0383 721445

147

Members of the group which prepared the guidance

Peter Cox OBE
Chairman
Recently retired Principal of Dartington College of Arts; Chairman of South West Arts and of Arts Share South West Trust

Sir Alec Atkinson
Vice-Chairman of the Committee of Inquiry

Peter Coles
Psychologist; Author of *The Manchester Hospital Arts Project and Art in the National Health Service* a report by the DHSS; recently carried out an assessment of the British Museum 'Please Touch' Exhibition

Stephen Lacey
Senior lecturer in film and drama at Bulmershe College, Reading; has experience of community theatre, community arts and drama with handicapped people

Lawrence Mackintosh
Head of Secretariat, Arts Council of Great Britain

Bert Massie OBE
Executive Assistant to the Director, RADAR (Royal Association for Disability and Rehabilitation); interested in physical disability and access, mobility and employment

Seona Reid
Director of Shape, a London-based organisation which promotes and encourages involvement in the arts by people with disabilities and special needs; Trustee of Artsline and Arts Access; Member of Executive Committee of Greater London Arts

Christina McDonald
(Organising Secretary)
Project Officer of the Committee of Inquiry

148

Appendix 8

Arts training in Scotland

A survey of opportunities for disabled students

The above survey was carried out in November and December 1983 to discover to what extent professional training in the arts in Scotland is open to students with disabilities.

Visits were made to the six colleges of higher education providing full-time degree or diploma level courses in drama, music or the visual arts. Where schools of architecture share premises with colleges included in the main survey, preliminary enquiries were also made about architecture training. A seventh institution was surveyed which provides specialist music training for school age children.

Discussions were held with administrative and faculty staff and, at one college, with disabled students.

Topics discussed included:

- college policies towards disabled applicants and students taking courses;

- demand for places by disabled students and difficulties experienced by them when taking courses;

- disablement among college staff and staff contact with students with disabilities;

- the accessibility of residential and study blocks and of course-work to disabled students;

- information about the needs of disabled people and contact with organisations representing their interests.

Policy

Only one of the institutions surveyed had a written policy on disabled applicants or students on courses. Five others said they treated applications from intending disabled students sympathetically. Most were prepared to relax academic criteria where appropriate but all insisted on the need to adhere to existing artistic criteria. It was recommended that colleges discuss the creation of a policy on disabled students and make a commitment to include this topic yearly on the agenda of the governing body.

Demand for places

All the institutions agreed that the number of disabled applicants was very small, with the number of disabled students attending at that time standing at just over 0.3% of the student population. A number of possible reasons for this were put forward and while it was agreed that any intending student of art, music, drama, etc who is otherwise sufficiently talented to undertake training should not be disqualified simply because he or she is disabled, in practice staff acknowledged a number of difficulties in implementing this which require further investigation and discussion.

Disablement and staff

In the seven institutions only three faculty staff members were identified as being disabled. A slightly larger number of ancillary and technical staff had disabilities.

Only one institution had identified a channel through which the needs of disabled students could be looked after, other than the normal ones, eg departmental head, domestic bursar. From discussion with disabled students, it seemed clear that thought should be given by college authorities as to methods of facilitating exchange between staff and disabled students about the needs and problems of both.

Access

In general, older buildings were found to be more difficult of access than newer ones. However, even buildings designed since 1970 often presented considerable access problems for disabled users. It was felt that more applications would come from disabled students if access facilities were improved, while access facilities might be improved more quickly if there were more disabled students. The situation remains static for a number of reasons which include lack of money for capital expenditure, lack of official awareness of what needs disabled students have, and lack of the will to change things.

All the colleges said that, to a certain extent, they could either direct disabled students towards those parts of the course with which they could cope or, if necessary, modify the course requirements to suit them. From discussions with disabled students it seemed that mostly they made subject choices based on what they felt they could manage. Reductions in staff ratios make it hard for colleges to give disabled students who do need extra attention the assistance they require. Awareness that their position is unusual makes disabled students unwilling to cause inconvenience by expressing their difficulties.

Information and contact

Regular contact between colleges and national bodies representing the interests of disabled people was disappointingly rare, which may indicate lack of activity on the part of both the colleges and the national organisations.

Student contact with disabled people relied for the most part on the inititatives of individual departments or students. It was considered that establishing regular channels of contact could lead to more sustained and developing relationships between colleges and groups in the community and thus counteract the loss of impetus caused by the changing student population and, to some extent, staff departures.

Architecture students were taught about the statutory regulations affecting disabled people. There was, however, no evidence that arts colleges in general taught students about the needs of disabled people as part of arts courses.

Alexander Dunbar

Note:

Copies of the full report 'Arts Training in Scotland' can be ordered from the Carnegie UK Trust, Comely Park House, Dunfermline, Fife.
Tel: 0383 721445

Appendix 9

'Arts for Everyone'

Guidance on provision for disabled people

The book is a practical guide for those running arts venues on how to provide opportunities that can enable disabled people to participate in arts activities of all kinds with the maximum of ease.

Managers of arts venues wishing to improve their services for disabled people have difficulty finding the required information. *Arts for Everyone* makes such information readily available in a precise form. The book includes chapters on modification to buildings, and on technical aids which will be essential for all kinds of arts buildings. Other chapters deal with particular kinds of arts events and activities: cinemas, theatres, museums, historic buildings, etc. New ideas for involving disabled people in these various forms of arts activities are set out.

Arts for Everyone draws together facts and figures, names and ideas which will enable all those involved in the arts world to expand and develop their services in ways which are sensitive to the needs and wishes of people with disabilities.

If the book has a message or theme it is that improvements which may be of particular benefit to disabled people are often better for everyone. There are many examples of experiments to serve the needs of a particular disabled group having resulted in permanent developments in arts provision, to the advantage of all and the enrichment of the arts in general.

Discovery rooms and tactile exhibitions, often started with the needs of visually handicapped visitors in mind, are rapidly developing into a new way of experiencing museum objects for everyone - eg a tactile exhibition of contemporary sculpture currently being presented at the Castle Museum, Nottingham in conjunction with the Arts Council of Great Britain.

Sign language interpretation of public guided tours is another way of incorporating hearing impaired visitors into museum activities - eg the British Museum has a monthly sign language interpreted gallery talk. Travelling exhibitions, mobile theatre and concerts are other ways of bringing the arts into hospitals and residential homes.

Anne Pearson

Note:

Arts for Everyone ISBN 0 903976 15 3 is due to be published in May 1985. Copies may be ordered from the Centre on Environment for the Handicapped, 126 Albert Street, London NW1. Tel: 01 267 6001

Appendix 10

Glossary of selected terms and acronyms

(acronyms are included only if separated from the full version in the text of the report)

Access committees - committees concerned with access problems affecting disabled people.

Adult education - post-school education which is mainly non-formal, but may be vocational or non-vocational.

Adult Training Centre - Local centre for training and rehabilitation of physically and mentally ill people. Usually administered by local authorities.

Arts for Everyone - guidance notes on how to make things easier for disabled people at arts venues. *(See Appendix 9)*.

Arts therapist - a professional who uses an arts medium within a therapeutic framework as the basis for clinical or social treatment. An *art therapist* uses the visual arts in this context.

Arts workshops - the group practice of arts techniques. Thus, in *theatre workshops* a group of people practise acting techniques and explore issues, situations, events and ideas through drama games, voice exercises, mime and so on.

BBC - British Broadcasting Corporation.

British Standards Institution - authority for the preparation and publication of national standards for industrial and consumer products.

CEEFAX, Prestel, Oracle, Viewdata - Television subtitle and information services.

Centre on Environment for the Handicapped - A London-based centre now administering the Access Committee for England.

DHSS - Department of Health and Social Security (in Great Britain). Department of Health and Social Services (in Northern Ireland).

Disability - any restriction or lack (resulting from an impairment) of ability to perform an activity in the manner or within the range considered normal for a human being (World Health Organisation definition). In this report *disablement* is used in the same general sense.

Disability Alliance - a charity which aims to help and support disabled people, and to promote research and legislative reform on their behalf.

DLF - Disabled Living Foundation, London.

Equity - Actors union of Great Britain incorporating the Variety Artistes Federation.

Further education - post-school education other than 'higher education'.

Gateway Clubs - A national network of social and recreational clubs for mentally handicapped people. Linked to MENCAP.

Handicap - a disadvantage for a given individual, resulting from an impairment or disability, that limits or prevents the fulfilment of a role that is normal, depending on age, sex, social and cultural factors, for that individual (World Health Organisation definition).

Higher education - education given in universities and in advanced courses in polytechnics or certain other establishments.

Hospices - Intensive care units, many of which are charitably supported, which provide care and support for the terminally ill and their families.

Impairment - any loss or abnormality of psychological, physiological or anatomical structure or function (World Health Organisation definition).

IBA - Independent Broadcasting Authority.

ILR - Independent Local Radio.

ITV - Independent Television.

Marks and Spencer - leading retail company with a patronage policy to assist community developments.

MENCAP - Royal Society for Mentally Handicapped Adults and Children.

National Health Service - State health service in the United Kingdom.

Outset - a charity which aims to encourage and enable young people to participate in voluntary activities, and to work with disabled people.

PHAB - Physically Handicapped and Able-Bodied Clubs.

RAA - Regional Arts Association.

RADAR - Royal Association for Disability and Rehabilitation.

RHA - Regional Health Authority.

RNIB - Royal National Institute for the Blind.

RNID - Royal National Institute for the Deaf.

SAC - Scottish Arts Council

SCAD - Scottish Committee for Arts and Disability, now established as a full committee of the Scottish Council on Disability under the title *SCD Committee on Arts for Scotland*.

SCD - Scottish Council on Disability.

Shape - A network of 14 independent but associated services operating in different parts of the United Kingdom (sometimes under the name *Artlink* or *Artshare*) whose purpose it is to link artists and arts companies with organisations and institutions for disabled or disadvantaged people. *Interlink* gives the Shape concept an international dimension.

Stoke Mandeville Hospital - A district general hospital in the Oxford area in which there is a spinal unit of 120 beds providing treatment and rehabilitation for spinal injury patients.

SWET - Society of West End Theatres.

Winged Fellowship Trust - a charity providing holidays and holiday centres for severely physically handicapped people.

Writer-in-residence - Professional writer ususally sponsored by an Arts Council or Association and attached to a school or arts venue. Similar programmes exist for other artists.

Index

Statutes, Orders and Regulations will be found together under Acts of Parliament

155

£4·95 net in UK only

ISBN 0 7199 1145 1

Published for
Carnegie UK Trust by
BEDFORD SQUARE PRESS I NCVO
26 Bedford Square,
London WC1B 3HU

This report of the committee of inquiry set up by the Carnegie UK Trust in 1982, under the chairmanship of Sir Richard Attenborough, is the first comprehensive review of facilities in the United Kingdom which enable disabled people to involve themselves in the arts. The committee found much excellent work being done by both public and private bodies, and much more that needs doing if disabled people are to play their full part in arts activities. Recommendations are made concerning access and availability, arts therapies, education and training, and employment opportunities.
'It lies within our power,' says Sir Richard Attenborough in his Preface, 'to transform the lives of disabled people and to enrich the world of art itself by their greater involvement.'
This report is designed to chart the way ahead.

ISBN 0-7199-1145-1

9 780719 911453

Cover design by Rachel Griffin
Cover photograph by
Michael Dyer Associates